Great Western Railway Halts

The peculiarly named Erconwald halt on the 'Ealing and Shepherds Bush Railway', nearly complete in 1920. Note low platforms and conductor rails about to be laid. The name presumably relates to Erconwald Road nearby; prior to opening the place became East Acton Station – a Halt no more. Not that it ever was, though the case is a reasonable illustration of the problems (and delights) of Halts, Haltes and Platforms.

Great Western Railway Halts

By Kevin Robertson

GWR

Volume 1

IRWELL
PRESS

ACKNOWLEDGEMENTS

Without the help and assistance of a number of persons none of this could have been written and as ever I am grateful to: David Abbott for valued asistance and restful transport!, British Rail and in particular Ian Coulson and Ian McNulty, Roger Carpenter, Michael Farr, The Great Western Society and in particular Lawrence Waters, Michael Hale, Mike Jolly, Phillip Kelley, the Keeper of Public Records at Kew, David Postle, Lens of Sutton, the staff at the National Railway Museum Library, Roger Simmonds, Jim and Mary Squelch — especially as it was a particularly difficult time for them, Paul Strong, Brian Hilton, Peter Squibb, and of course George and Chris for encouragement and support throughout. One day even they might become GWR enthusiasts!

Aside from the books and other items referred to within the text the following have been consulted as source references: *GWR Atlas* — R.A. Cooke, Pub. Wild Swan, *Track Plans of GWR and BRW* — R.A. Cooke, *A Register of GWR Halts* — C. Clinker *Clinker's Register of Closed Stations England and Wales,* GWR Working and Public Timetables, *Locomotives of the GWR Parts 1-13* — Pub. RCTS *Locomotives of the LSWR* by D.L. Bradley — Pub. RCTS, Minute books and Records of the GWR held at the Public Record Office, *Great Western Magazine,* Board of Trade reports of Inspection *Private and Untimetabled Railway Stations* — Godfrey Croughton R.W. Kidner Alan Young — Pub. Oakwood.

CONTENTS

Published by

Irwell Press

3 Durley Avenue, Pinner, Middlesex, HA5 1JQ.

Printed by Amadeus Press, Huddersfield

PREFACE

For the student of Great Westernry – with apologies to T.W.E.Roche – the bookshelves are fortunately well stocked with a variety of subjects, from locomotives to the most obscure branch line, with the present writer only too aware of his own offerings.

Pore over almost any of these publications and it will not be too long before a photograph is found of ' ..... Halt', the like of which abounded on the system; to date they have been relatively ignored by the railway writer.

At this stage it may be appropriate to recount briefly the sequence of events leading up to the compilation of this record. It began some years back when I was privileged to be invited by BR to join in the sifting and classification of archive documents, prior to their transfer to the Public Record Office. Amongst these was a *GWR Register of Halts,* a document I had certainly never previously encountered; it revealed a number of locations designated 'halt', yet this suffix had not been carried. Closer examination uncovered further anomalies and yet here they were in an official publication – accuracy then guaranteed!

The original intention then was to simply reproduce this document, with an illustration of each stopping place. This though was quickly deemed impractical, as well as almost impossible, for some locations were hardly ever, it seemed, visited by the railway photographer. There were other dis-advantages, for a number of halts existed prior to and subsequent to the listing and accordingly would be omitted. Instead the next move was the compilation of a register of all GWR and associated halts (that is, the absorbed lines) up to 31st December 1947. BR events therefore, such as new halts, downgraded stations and renamings are not included. It has been necessary, however, to include a number of photographs taken after 1948.

To include BR information would have involved tedious repetition of closure dates, which in themselves could have become no doubt depressing. To make up for this I have included in the listings known information relating to all private and untimetabled halts as well as proposed sites, a number of which I'm sure will be new to the reader.

In compiling this book many sources of information were used but in particular I would like to acknowledge the invaluable help of two publications – the excellent registers produced by Charles Clinker and Ron Cooke's fine Atlas and series of track plans. Without frequent recourse to these volumes this record could not have been completed.

It has been a pleasure also to diverge into the initial steam railmotor services as well as, at last, (I hope) defining the differences between a 'Halt' and a 'Platform' – or should I say 'Halte'?

Following an initial explanatory section the listing in this first volume runs alphabetically, A to L, including illustrations and schematic track plans wherever possible. Other sources of information and further reading on any particular site has also been included under each location. My apologies to any author, who like this one has had acknowledgement of his own efforts omitted in the work of others.

Space and practicalities preclude an illustration of every stopping place for although I try and maintain a good relationship with the publisher I do not think even they would take kindly to a volume with 800-plus illustrations ...

Volume 2 covering halts and platforms M to Y is now in preparation and I would be grateful for any additional views for inclusion in it. Should anyone care to submit any further information, amendment and/or corrections to the present work I would be delighted to receive it.

The Great Western had, with the introduction of the 'Halt', made a determined effort to tackle the competition from road transport at a very early stage. It was in effect the model for an early form of transport integration, intended to serve local needs by utilising existing facilities to the best effect. Indeed this very point was seized upon by no less a person than Colonel Yorke of the Board of Trade in 1903 who stated ....

My own view is that every attempt to get the greatest possible use out of a railway should be encouraged....

It is a matter of regret therefore that successive governments have for years failed to heed such wise advice, for ninety years on the Colonel's words still ring true – overcrowded roads, congested cities and rising pollution. Perhaps someone may yet listen.

Kevin Robertson,

Eastleigh, 1990.

*See later for the full draft of Colonel Yorke's report.

Private and not for Publication.

GREAT WESTERN RAILWAY

LIST OF HALTS.

This List has been prepared with the intention of making it easy for members of the Staff to give information as to the situation of Halts on the Railway.

R. H. NICHOLLS,
SUPERINTENDENT OF LINE,
PADDINGTON STATION.

June, 1928.

PLACE.	SITUATED BETWEEN.
Aber Junction	Caerphilly and Penyrheol.
rAberangell	Cemmes Road and Dinas Mawddwy.
rAbercwmboi	Mountain Ash and Aberaman.
Aberffrwd	Aberystwyth and Devil's Bridge.
*Aberthin	Cowbridge and Ystradowen.
Alberta Place	Penarth Town and Lower Penarth.
Alford	Castle Cary and Keinton Mandeville.
Alphington	Exeter (St. Thomas) and Ide.
Ammanford Colliery	Ammanford and Glanamman.
Arddleen	Four Crosses and Pool Quay.
Ashton Gate	Clifton Bridge and Bedminster.
rAston Botterell	Stottesdon and Burwarton.
Aston Cantlow	Bearley and Great Alne.
Avoncliff	Freshford and Bradford-on-Avon.
Aynho Park	Kings Sutton and Ardley.
rBacton	Abbeydore and Vowchurch.
rBaldwins	Danygraig and Jersey Marine.
Baptist End	Windmill End and Blowers Green.
Beanacre	Chippenham and Melksham.
Beavers Hill	Manorbier and Lamphey.
Beddau	Llantwit and Cross Inn.
Berw Road	Pontypridd and Cilfynydd.
rBerwig	Coed Poeth and Minera.
rBittaford	Wrangaton and Ivybridge.
*Black Lion Crossing	Dare Junction and Cwmaman Colliery.
Black Rock	Portmadoc and Criccieth.
Blaenplwyf	Lampeter and Aberayron.
Bledlow Bridge	Princes Risborough and Chinnor.
Bolham	Tiverton and Bampton.
Boughton	Henwick and Bransford Road.
Bowbridge Crossing	Brimscombe and Stroud.
rBoxford	Newbury and Lambourn.
rBrampford Speke	Thorverton and Stoke Canon.
Brentham (for North Line)	Park Royal and Greenford.
Brimley	Heathfield and Bovey.
Brimscombe Bridge	Brimscombe and Stroud.
Brockmoor	Brettell Lane and Himley.
rBromham and Rowde	Seend and Devizes.
Bromley	Brettell Lane and Himley.
Broughton Gifford	Melksham and Holt Junction.
rBrymbo West Crossing	Brymbo and Coed Poeth.
Bryngwyn	Llanfechain and Llanfyllin.

*Not in use at present.   r Parcels dealt with.

A halt being built, at an unknown location. From the position of the wagons it may well be that widening is taking place though there is a platform only on one side of the line. Why this should be so is unclear. Around the gutter line of the 'pagoda' there is evidence of an ornate form of ironwork, which appeared on a number of early halts. Such fittings were generally removed in later years. As a general rule all new passenger facilities had to be inspected and certified by the Board of Trade, later the Railway Inspectorate. From the surviving files it would appear that this was not always the case.

National Railway Museum

'HALT, HALTE, OR PLATFORM?'

Synonymous with the Great Western were a number of features which, according to its supporters at least, helped keep the company in the forefront of railway development, both in this country and overseas. In detailing these features it is tempting to refer solely to Swindon Works and the standard range of locomotives produced by Churchward. In so doing, however, the seemingly less glamorous yet equally important work of the other departments could easily be overlooked. For example, were it not for the development of Automatic Train Control by the Signal Department then the achievements of the locomotives would have been all the poorer. Similarly, the various cut–off lines built under the direction of the Chief Civil Engineer had reduced journey times between the major centres.

It would be difficult in this short work to do real justice to the achievements of the CME, the CSE and the CCE in the early part of this century. Many books have already covered much of this ground including, even, the work of the Chief Goods Manager and Docks departments. However, the Traffic Department, which oversaw the promotion and development of services throughout the system, is little covered. The level of its success may be gauged by a glimpse at the traffic statistics (see appendix) and it would not be difficult to conclude that failure in this department would have had catastrophic financial effects on the company.

The Edwardian era had seen the beginnings of a general change in attitudes, following years of restricted High Victorian ideals. Allied to this was a technological revolution, not least in the form of the motor car, something the GWR was quick to recognise as a major threat. There is little to betray this in the general Minutes and records, though these are notoriously unforthcoming – perhaps small developments, such ventures as the proposed Stroud District and Cheltenham Tramway were considerations. What can be certain, however, is that the GWR attempted to garner additional traffic and to this end the collaboration of a number of departments was necessary. The result was the opening of numerous 'Haltes' and 'Platforms', served both by ordinary trains as well as the new steam railmotors.

At this stage it may perhaps be appropriate to attempt a definition of the differences between a Halte and a Platform. Thomas B. Peacock in his *Great Western London Suburban Services* (Oakwood Press):

> The word 'station' carried a well recognised connotation throughout the nineteenth century. A station was equipped to deal with most classes of traffic, handled by a staff presided over by a stationmaster. Because of the need to hold one or more trains at a station for widely varying periods, it was convenient to integrate the station with the block post. But with the advent of the rail–car came the 'halt', exclusive to it and an altogether new kind of stopping–place, without staff and without signals. Simultaneously, the rapid development of local services brought the need for designating a stopping–place intermediate in status between a halt and a station; and for this purpose the word 'Platform' was coined. Unlike most halts, Platforms were long enough to accommodate such trains as would normally call there. Platforms, too were not necessarily linked to signal sections but most had a staff of one, possibly two, and included a booking office. Whilst many stopping–places were built as Platforms from the outset, others had been raised from the status of halt. As the years passed, however, the Company made little, if any, attempt to educate the public in the use of the term 'Platform'. Halts that had been converted to Platforms continued to be designated as halts, and stopping places that should have been referred to as Platforms were classed as stations. Yet, surprisingly the word continued to make a haphazard appearance in the public time books up to 1947....

The Halt therefore was to provide intermediate stopping places between stations served by self contained vehicles upon which tickets would be issued by a conductor. The word Halte was copied from the contemporary French although the 'e' was quickly dispensed with. This did not take place however until at least a few sites opened with it firmly in place on the nameboard. Fortunately a number a photographs have survived showing this feature.

Such a simple explanation may deserve further elaboration and indeed a number of questions immediately arise. As is well known, continental railways have long been exponents of the roadside railway, passengers boarding the trains from ground level. Despite the passing of Light Railway Acts within Great Britain little use was made of the relaxed conditions. The advent of the Halte and railmotor service then, could be seen as an attempt to provide improved facilities within the framework of an existing system.

The ticket window at The Miners Arms, located underneath the 'pub water tank.' In charge in 1929 was Thomas Henry Dando, the notice reading 'Passengers requiring tickets up to 7 p.m. on weekdays are requested to ring the bell. After that time and on Sundays Passengers without tickets should notify the Guard on joining the Train.'

LGRP

Relations with France at this time were not at their best; there was dislike and even mistrust of the French and their behaviour and this may in part explain the rapid alteration in spelling of the word Halte, in favour of the English version. Such mistrust certainly did not prevail in all departments of the GWR, for was it not Churchward himself who in 1903 took delivery of a 4-4-2 compound engine to the design of De Glehn?

Back in England the half yearly shareholders meeting held at Paddington, on 13th August 1903, had heard the Chairman, Lord Cawdor, announce in general terms the company's future ideas for rail motor car services. Meanwhile the traffic department had deliberated upon a suitable first location for the venture, and as is well documented a site between Stroud and Stonehouse was selected. No doubt lurking in the minds of the Traffic Department managers was a pre-emptive strike` against the proposed tramway here. Accordingly preliminary plans were prepared as well as notification given to the various interested parties. One of these was the Stroud Rural District Council who were far from enthusiastic about the project. Indeed such was the opposition that it was moved to write to the Railway Inspectorate at The Board of Trade.....

That the Stroud RDC, having been informed that the GWR Company have announced their intention of running motor cars in between the ordinary passenger and goods trains on the portion of the line between Chalford and Stonehouse (the greater part of which is in the Rural District of Stroud) desire to call to the attention of the Board of Trade to the following facts.

1. Between Chalford and Stonehouse there are 12 level crossings on the GWR.

2. It is suggested that at some of these level crossings the motor car will stop to take up and set down passengers.

The Stroud RDC respectfully submit to the Board of Trade that if the Board sanction the running of motor cars as suggested they should insist that at each of the 12 level crossings above mentioned there should be either a bridge over the line or an attendant to open and close gates and prevent danger to the public and they also respectfully suggest that at any crossings where it is proposed motor cars should stop there should be a small station or other protection to the public to prevent people who are waiting for or alighting from motor cars being endangered by other trains passing on the line....

For his part Colonel Yorke of the Board of Trade added his own comments. They are of particular interest, not only for his views regarding the Stroud RDC proposals but for the comparison one can draw with congestion on the roads today......

The Board of Trade report they have had correspondence with the GWR on the subject who state they did not anticipate any objection from the Board of Trade. The GWR intend to work the cars under the usual block rules – additional 'block boxes' being erected if necessary.* In this way the Board of Trade are within their rights ..... where the company require assistance is in the matter of intermediate stations or stopping places. It is proposed to stop the cars at the cross roads and other places for the purpose of picking up or setting down passengers and the Company do not wish to be compelled to erect station buildings, high platforms, lavatories etc, or to have anyone in charge of each stopping place. These stopping places will not be used by long trains other then the motor cars and will be devoted solely to local purposes. I expressed the opinion that if these places were not advertised as stations in Bradshaw they could be treated in the same way as golf platforms and workmens platforms, several of which have been passed by the Board of Trade and buildings could be dispensed with.

I put the above unofficial conversation on record because the question is now brought before the department officially by this letter from the Stroud RDC and the policy of the department towards this proposal and others of a similar nature has to be decided....

My own view is that every attempt to get the greatest possible use out of a railway should be encouraged.

It is probable that the instigation of these intermediate stopping places will encourage trespassing and may cause an increase of accidents to trespassers and others crossing the railway – perhaps too would-be passengers, but it seems unavoidable.

At any rate this is a matter over which the Stroud RDC has no responsibility. I take it that the level crossings herein referred to are occupation crossings or footpaths. If so wicket gates or turnstiles will be required to afford access to the line.

A rare view of the original railmotor shed at Chalford, which opened in 1903 with the Stroud – Stonehouse service. The building is believed to have measured 75ft by 15ft and was probably of corrugated iron construction. It was pulled down around 1935.

S.J. Gardiner Collection

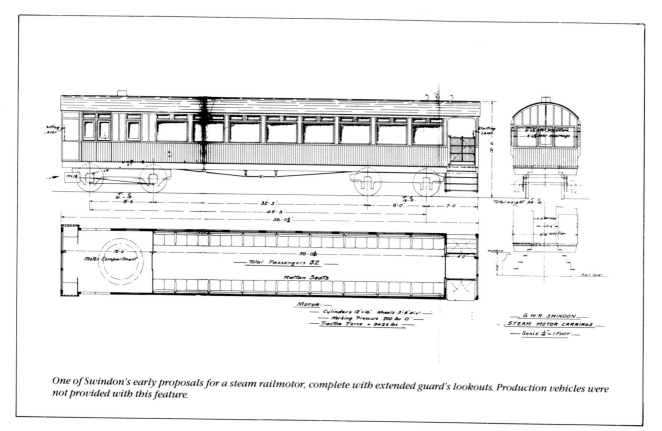

One of Swindon's early proposals for a steam railmotor, complete with extended guard's lookouts. Production vehicles were not provided with this feature.

But whether public level crossing or private, the provision of buildings does not seem to be necessary or even useful. At any rate this is a matter to be dealt with by the Board of Trade after inspection.

It is disappointing to find a local authority raising objections to the proposal to afford the public increased facilities for locomotion.....

Sir Francis Hopwood, President of the Board of Trade added his comments agreeing with Colonel Yorke.

The way was now clear for the GWR to commence their new service, for which Churchward designed the first of his steam railmotor vehicles. These have been expounded upon in several books dealing specifically with the subject – see acknowledgements, and now is not the time to repeat the information. Suffice it to say that Churchward had decided upon the suitability of a steam railmotor design following trials around Stroud with a borrowed LSWR/LBSCR vehicle.

The actual vehicle borrowed was No.1, and the understanding is that it was moderately successful. This in itself is rather surprising as research by the present writer (*The Southsea Branch*, Kingfisher 1985) unearthed evidence that the joint vehicles, Nos. 1 & 2, were not only underpowered in service and incapable of hauling a trailing load but that this had been evident very early on during trials. It must be a matter of some considerable thought then as to how No.1 managed to acquit itself satisfactorily over the steeply graded lines around Stroud. The simple answer may possibly be that Churchward recognised the potential of such a vehicle rather then its performance on the trial. There is no evidence to suggest that the later built Swindon machines were afflicted so severely by the shortcomings of the 'prototypes'.

The steam railmotors were themselves to be supplemented and later superseded by the auto-train but it is worth referring briefly to the fact that at least one alternative design of steam railmotor was prepared at Swindon prior to construction of the first vehicles. This proposal showed a

vehicle carried on two four wheel bogies – one of which was the power bogie – with an overall length of just over 56ft. Matchboard sides were envisaged with the unusual addition of guard's lookouts. The latter feature was not perpetuated in the main production design.

On 22nd July 1903, the Great Western wrote to the Board of Trade advising them of their intentions.....

> Sir,
>
> It is the intention of this Company to run a series of Steam Motor Cars intermingled with the ordinary train service between Chalford and Stonehouse stations, on the Swindon and Gloucester line. At the outset the motor cars will run between 7.00 a.m. and 9.00 p.m. affording approximately an hourly service in each direction.
>
> A tracing accompanying this letter shows the type of car it is proposed to use. It will be open from end to end with side seats for 52 passengers, an end door opening to a gangway with side steps suitable for platform or rail level, and collapsible gates and capable of being driven from either end.
>
> Besides stopping at the existing stations it is proposed these cars shall call at intermediate stopping places between the stations, to take up and set down passengers as described below.
>
> Chalford to Brimscombe; intermediate stopping place to be St. Mary's Crossing.
>
> Brimscombe to Stroud; intermediate stopping place to be Ham Mill Crossing.
>
> Stroud and Stonehouse Stations; intermediate stopping place to be Cains Cross.**

*No additional signal boxes were in fact found necessary along this section at this time.

**There is no record of a stopping place with the name Cains Cross being opened. Between Stroud and Stonehouse there were three intermediate halts, Downfield Crossing, Cashes Green Halt, and Ebley Crossing. Of these the first and last-named were amongst the first opened, on 12th October 1903, though neither is near the 103¼ milepost referred to in the text. Instead, at this point Cashes Green Halt

(continued from page 3)

was opened in 1930. It may be concluded then that a stopping place at Cains Cross – Cashes Green was envisaged in 1903 but for an unknown reason was not proceeded with. Intermediate stopping places were provided at the other two locations. When in 1930 a halt was agreed for milepost 103¼ an alternative to the original name was also decided upon. Interestingly the name 'Cainscross Bridge' is referred to in the statement of traffic for January 1904.

At St. Mary's and Ham Mill Crossings, gatemen are employed and landing places will be provided by levelling the ballast on either side of the line so that, by means of side steps, passengers may conveniently enter and leave the cars at the rail level. Passengers entering and leaving the cars at the two level crossings will be looked after by the gateman and those who may require to cross the railway will only be permitted to pass over the ordinary crossing between the crossing gates.

It is proposed to provide an intermediate stopping place near the 103¼ mile post to serve Cains Cross and adjacent villages. At this site landing places on the rail level will be provided with footways up the embankment, steps to the roadway on each side of an overbridge and pathways along the embankment from the short platforms to a foot crossing 80 yards from the overbridge. With these facilities it will be unnecessary for passengers travelling by the motor car to cross the lines at Cains Cross. Ordinary trains will not call there.

At Stonehouse it will be necessary, in order to facilitate the working of motor cars, after the arrival of a car at the down platform to reload it at that platform for the 'up' journey. To comply with the requirements of the Board of Trade in this respect a locking bar will be provided at the cross over road which become facing points to cars starting on the' up' journey from the 'down' platform at Stonehouse. The motor car will of course, when occupying the running lines be treated as an ordinary train and signalled under the ordinary Block Telegraph system.

In the circumstances mentioned I beg to ask that exemption of the ordinary requirements of the Board of Trade may be given in respect of:
1. Raised platforms at the intermediate stopping places.
2. Passengers conveniences and shelters at the intermediate stopping places.
3. Signals at the intermediate stopping places.

The early extension of similar motor car services to other sections of the line is contemplated.

I am Sir.....

The Board of Trade were thus moved to resolve the matter one way or the other. Surprisingly no written record of this survives in the files although it is evident that the decision was positive for the motor car service was put into effect from Monday 12th October 1903. In a somewhat novel departure *The Times* reported on the new service a few days earlier, on 8th October 1903.† The newspaper reported that Board of Trade permission for the new venture had been obtained and that it was proposed to run an hourly service in each direction calling at St. Mary's Crossing, Brimscombe Station, Ham Mill Crossing, Stroud Station, Downfield Crossing and Ebley Crossing.

Two days later, on 10th October *The Times* wrote further reporting a press trip held the previous day and run '...in beautiful weather .... and completely successful.' Mention was also made of some of those travelling, which included several senior officers from the GWR, Messrs. C. Aldington, G.J.Churchward, W. Dawson, Marillier and Waister.

Presumably the Stroud RDC had now conceded defeat, for no evidence has surfaced regarding further complaint; the full steam railmotor service commenced on Monday 12th October 1903 and was inspected by Colonel Yorke shortly afterwards on 27th October:

.....I have inspected the arrangements in connection with the steam motor car service which has been established by the GWR Company between Chalford and Stonehouse stations on the Swindon and Gloucester section of their line.

The motor cars have two four wheel bogies, the engine and boiler being at one end and a gangway by which passengers enter and leave the car at the other. The boiler which is vertical is carried upon the bogie truck below it. It is not connected in any way to the floor or framework of the car which is built around it. The engine, which is attached to the same bogie has two small horizontal cyl-

†The GWR was not the first to use steam railmotors on branch lines, the joint LSWR/LBSCR East Southsea line from Fratton commencing such a service from 1st June 1903. 'Steam carriages,' where the locomotive unit was permanently attached to a carriage portion had been designed and run elsewhere although not on the basis of providing a service to intermediate stopping places designated 'halts' or 'platforms.'

One of the GWR buses in the Stroud area – the Chalford service on its first day, 1st March 1905. This particular route expired in a little over three months, a similar fate befalling the other Great Western buses in the area

Lens of Sutton

inders and bogie wheels are coupled. The car is 57ft long from end to end (excluding buffers) and the passenger compartment is 38ft 7inches long affording accommodation for 52 passengers.

There is only one class, viz 3rd. The wheels are fitted with the automatic vacuum brake and hand brake, and there is a regulator handle and handles for both brakes at each end of the car. The car can thus be driven in the usual manner from either end and the driver is invariably placed at the leading end of the car. This is an important detail as I regard it essential for the safety both of passengers in the car and of the public at level crossings and of men working on the line – that the person in charge of the motive machinery should always be stationed at the leading end of the car and should so long as he is in charge of the machinery have no other duties to perform.

There are four existing stations on the section served by the motor car, viz, Chalford, Brimscombe, Stroud and Stonehouse, and four additional stopping places have been provided at public level crossings viz, St Mary's Crossing, Ham Mill Crossing, Downfield Crossing and Ebley Crossing, making a total of eight stopping places. The car can make 12 journeys each way daily with extra trips on Fridays and Saturdays.

It was originally proposed that platforms should not be provided at the level crossings and the Board of Trade consented to this arrangement on the condition that the car was fitted with steps to enable passengers to alight on the ground or enter the car with safety. The Company has however found it expedient to provide platforms 100ft long at each crossing as the picking up and discharge of passengers is therefore greatly accelerated.

These platforms are fenced at the back, have each two lamps and are connected by footpath with the adjacent road. The gatekeeper in charge of the level crossing looks after the platform. I am informed by the officers of the company that this motor car service has given great satisfaction and has so far been highly successful and I understand that further developments are in contemplation. The experiment is one which may, I submit, be regarded with appreciation.

I have the honour.....

Praise indeed then for the GWR and a complete change from the relationship between the Board of Trade and the company just a few years earlier, in the face of the railways' apparent apathy over the implementation of basic safety in working. (see *The Marlborough Branch*, Robertson and Abbott – Irwell Press)

The way was thus clear for a rapid expansion of both the 'Halt' and 'Platform' and with it the steam railmotor. Clinker provides some statistics on these which are listed in an appen-

dix. Figures have also been found giving details of the number of trains and railmotors using the line between Chalford and Stonehouse during the year ending 30th June 1904, based on an actual line survey carried out in September 1903 and January 1904:

	Pass.	Mtr.	Gds.
Tetbury Road Goods-Chalford	8688		12198
Chalford-St Marys Crossing	8688	5822	12198
St Marys Crossing-Brimscombe	8688	5832	12198
Brimscombe-Brimscombe Bge	8688	5832	12198
Brimscombe Bge-Ham Mill Crossing	8688	5832	12198
Ham Mill Crossing-Stroud	8688	5832	12198
Stroud-Downfield Crossing	8892	5815	12822
Downsfield Crossing-Cainscross Bge	8892	5815	12822
Cainscross Bge-Ebley Crossing	8892	5815	12822
Ebley Crossing-Stonehouse	8892	5815	12822
Stonehouse-Gloucester Sth Junc	8904		12822

The Company also attempted to develop services in other areas of the system by the provision of halts. Amongst these were the Plymouth/Cornwall district in 1904 and Wrexham in 1905. Oxford followed in 1908 although in this case the comparative success experienced elsewhere was not so apparent, and within a few years a number of the original stopping places had closed. Indeed the policy of closing unprofitable halts and platforms was to remain throughout the existence of the company, although on occasion changing fortunes allowed closed halts to reopen. Material recovered from some of the closed sites were occasionally used elsewhere, perhaps even many miles from the original location. Where this is known to have occurred details are given under the appropriate listing.

Meanwhile in 1904 the first true GWR 'Platform' was opened at Rodmarton, between Kemble and Culkerton. Stopping places of this nature also flourished from this time on, although certainly not in the same numbers as the 'Halts'. Indeed the GWR seemed at times unable to differentiate between one and the other and similarly the Taff Vale Railway designated all their sites 'Platforms' – an abbreviation of the phrase 'Motor Car Platform'. The neighbouring Rhymney Rail-

The 'typical' Great Western Halt, at Drybrook on the GWR Forest of Dean branch. Obviously intended to serve the local community – note the housing behind – such places prospered until the advance of the internal combustion engine.

Lens of Sutton

Though of indifferent quality the historical interest of this photograph warrants its inclusion, for it depicts a steam railmotor on the Chalford and Stonehouse service, paused at Downfield Crossing Halt. Certain of the first stopping places were built with low level or no platforms at all (note the standard height facilities here). Very likely this view dates from the period 1903 to 1914.

National Railway Museum

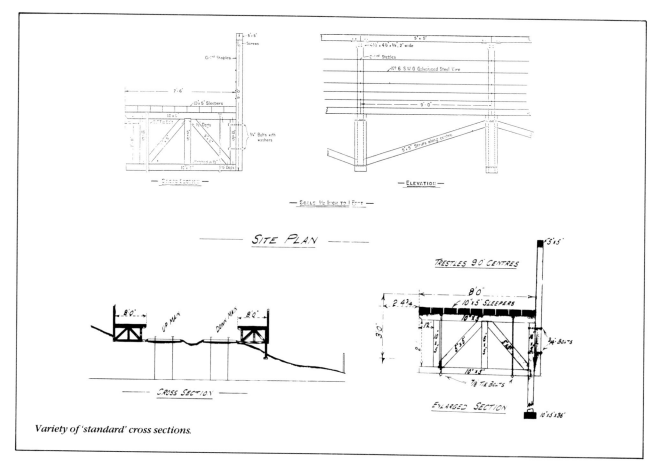

Variety of 'standard' cross sections.

way suffered from the same confusion, using 'Halt' for its stopping places. Bradshaw too seemed unable to define one from the other, for here all were termed 'Halts' which has no doubt led to further difficulties over the years.

Coterminous with the introduction of the halt (the term is used hereon in its loosest sense) and steam railmotor services came the road motor service which would eventually envelop the majority of the system. Again it would be tempting to digress into the area and aside from this brief mention the reader is referred to the veritable plethora of GWR branch line histories, usually detailing the road services. The standard works on the subject – *Railway Motor Bus & Bus Services 1902 – 33*, John Cummings and *GWR Road Vehicles*, Phillip Kelley OPC – are well worth a read.

Of course most reported information derives ultimately from official sources and is therefore somewhat unbalanced. 'Profit and loss' however, in the form of introduction and cessation of services, is usually coldly recorded – the trick is in the interpretation. That the halt venture and steam railmotors were popular can only be judged by their continued existence. Indeed expansion had continued unabated, at the expense, incidentally, of the unfortunate Stroud tramway, destined never to be built.

A letter on the subject of 'Indicators at Halts' was published in the December 1912 issue of the *Great Western Magazine*, headed 'A reader writes....'

To the general travelling public – who are but little acquainted with railway methods – it is somewhat confusing to know which is the up and which is the down platform at the various halts. In consequence, they run some risk in hurriedly crossing the line, on discovering, by an approaching car, that they are on the wrong platform. Also, sometimes intending

passengers, through some irregularity of their watches, or alteration of the time table, wait for some time for a car that has departed before their belated arrival at the halt. In order to obviate such uncertainties, I would suggest that boards, lettered 'up platform' and 'down platform' and an indicating appliance to show the departure time of the next car, be fixed at all halts. The appliance I have in mind would be similar to that used by the Post Office authorities at letter boxes, for showing the time of the next collection.....

Services at halts were at first largely worked by steam railmotors and it is interesting to consider the number of these units required for the daily service. By 1912 at least 153 halts, or platforms were open:

NUMBER OF STEAM RAILMOTOR CARS NEEDED FOR REGULAR DAILY SERVICE

Four weeks ended	Four weeks ended	Four weeks ended	Four weeks ended
27/1/12: 49	24/1/14: 50	23/1/15: 24	22/1/16: 31
24/2/12: 50	21/2/14: 49	20/2/15: 46	19/2/16: 30
23/3/12: 31	21/3/14: 48	20/3/15: 44	18/3/16: 30
20/4/12: 15	18/4/14: 49	17/4/15: 34	15/4/16: 29
18/5/12: 43	16/5/14: 48	15/5/15: 34	13/5/16: 28
15/6/12: 47	13/6/14: 50	12/6/15: 33	10/6/16: 29
13/7/12: 47	11/7/14: 50	10/7/15: 33	8/7/16: 29
10/8/12: 51	8/8/14: 52	7/8/15: 33	5/8/16: 28
7/9/12: 53	5/9/14: 51	4/9/15: 33	2/9/16: 27
5/10/12: 50	3/10/14: 50	2/10/15: 34	30/9/16: 26
2/11/12: 51	31/10/14: 48	30/10/15: 34	28/10/16: 26
30/11/12: 51	28/11/14: 47	27/11/15: 31	25/11/16: 28
28/12/12: 52	26/12/14: 49	25/12/15: 31	23/12/16: 29

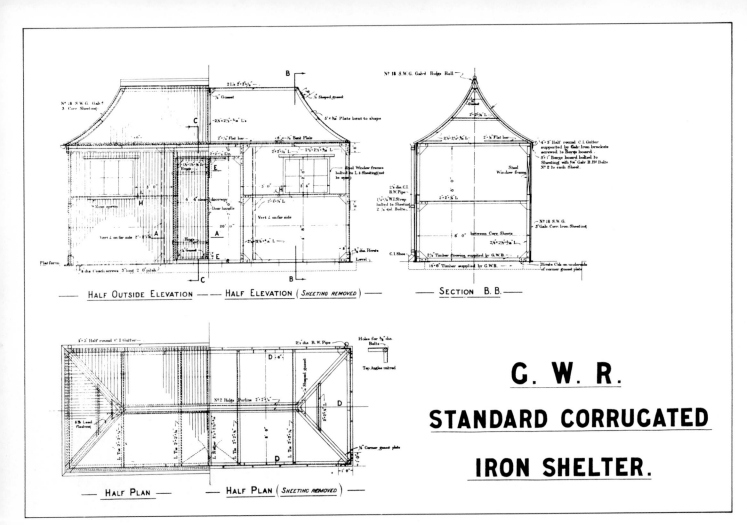

— HALF OUTSIDE ELEVATION — — HALF ELEVATION (*SHEETING REMOVED*) —   — SECTION B.B. —

— HALF PLAN — — HALF PLAN (*SHEETING REMOVED*) —

G. W. R.
STANDARD CORRUGATED
IRON SHELTER.

Compiled from official records, the gradual reduction in units required between 1914 and 1916 is clearly an indication of war-time cutbacks and shortage of manpower. For details of the services concerned the reader is referred to either the RCTS *Locomotives of the GWR Parts 11 & 13,* or the various company timetables, public and working, of the period.

Another development with the advent of the halt was the ticket agency. The majority of halts were unstaffed, although platforms usually had a 'Platform Attendant' in charge – the grade was later altered to that of a 'Grade 1 Porter'. Ticket agencies had of course been around for some years prior to 1903 – the earliest known site on the GWR commenced business in 1888 and the number increased dramatically after this date, with a standard sign available proclaiming, 'Tickets may be obtained from.....' These agents received a small commission on their sales, a notable one being the *Miners Arms* public house, at Farrington Gurney in Somerset. It is however very difficult to generalise on the subject of staffing levels at halts as there would appear to be innumerable exceptions. In addition changes occurred over the course of the years to co-incide with altered traffic needs.

It would be expected, perhaps, that a range of standard fittings were provided at what, after all, were ostensibly similar locations. In fact nothing could be further from the truth and the GWR, generally renowned for its efforts at standardisation, was unable to come up with a standard arrangement for its many halts. This evident lack of uniformity was quickly noticed by the Railway Inspectorate which commented as such in 1906, in the course of an official visit to Coryates Halt – see text. Perhaps as a result of the Board of Trade's report at this time it would appear the majority of halts opened subsequently were provided with the usual 3ft high platform. This

made them more suited for ordinary trains and thus more flexible. Some sites of course retained their low platforms to the end and it remained common practice that steam railmotors and auto trailers be equipped with steps, to be swung out when required. Certainly in later years a set of 'standard' instructions were issued regarding the facilities at halts, these being appended later.

How was a location selected as suitable for a halt? A number of factors would be considered; representation from the village council, market research, traffic flows etc., and on at least one occasion the suggestion of a member of staff (Hightown Halt)

It will be recalled that reference was made earlier in the text to the rapid closure of a halt or platform, should it prove uneconomic. In similar vein such changes affected stations, with a number being downgraded to halt status. Examples were Ide in Devon and Chedworth on the former MSWJ system. Conversely, there is at least one occasion (Cosford) where a former halt was extended and thus upgraded to a station.

A quick glance through the accompanying listings may in fact cause the reader to doubt certain entries. It should be pointed out that in most cases references are taken from the official publication of June 1928 marked 'Private and not for Publication' but entitled 'List of Halts – This list has been prepared with the intention of making it easy for members of staff to give more information as to the situation of Halts on the railway.'

Within its covers are listed nearly 500 halts extant in 1927 – far more than numbers suggested elsewhere. The reason is simply the broad designation, whatever the finer points of definition, applied by the GWR to a number of stopping

An early view of Defiance Platform, showing the replacement stopping place brought into use in May 1908. The alignment of the original railway can be seen through the arch. The use of three pagoda shelters is certainly unusual and is doubtless connected with the need to segregate officers from men. The photograph is looking west towards Saltash.

places. For example, stopping places on the former Cleobury Mortimer and Ditton Priors route were classed as halts. In fact most were little more then gravel mounds and thus fall easily and neatly within the classification. None on this line, however, actually carried the suffix, on board or notice. Similarly all but one of the stopping places on the Lambourn branch from Newbury were deemed halts; there is particular confusion with respect to this branch and only 'Newbury West Fields Halt' bore the title proper. On the other hand Welford Park did not; it was a simple crossing place, though it boasted signal cabin and goods yard! The old notion that the presence of a 'pagoda' shelter defined a halt is no longer tenable.

With the grouping in 1923 the GWR inherited a number of halts and platforms from other companies. Names were sometimes duplicated and were necessarily changed to avoid confusion. This is not to say that the GWR itself was without its own name problems; Defiance Halt and Defiance Platform – in the same area – was a good example. Some time later the problem arose again manifesting itself on this occasion in three Whitchurchs'!

A memorandum of 6th April 1922, from Grierson, Chief Engineer, throws light on the fact that even the GWR had become confused at the category of some stopping places.....

Some of the documents I am now receiving are for easements or works at Halts, the position of which are not indicated on my copy of the 2 chain survey. It will be a great convenience to me in connection with the indexing of the documents and also facilitate the search for the same, to know the precise position of the various Halts throughout the System and I shall be much obliged by your letting me know if you can arrange for this information to be shewn on the surveys I have...

Halt building seems generally to have proceeded in phases, with the final flourish taking place from 1927 to 1935. At the same time there were a number of closures, 31 in all, countered by 169 new halts. It may also be of interest to relate that at least 34 other closures of locations carrying the 'halt' or 'platform' suffix occurred during the period 1923 to 1947.

Around this time also there is evidence of true 'standard' facilities emerging, with new halts grouped in one of three classes, each of which could be subdivided 'a' or 'b'. Details of this are appended later.

The GWR were of course facing ever greater competition from road transport. Coupled with rising costs it would be fair to say that halts opened in this period were even more spartan than their predecessors. Difficulties then, were mounting, passing on to British Railways after Nationalisation and ultimately to the Beeching era of the early sixties.

Four Oaks, in June 1959, with the 4.8pm Gloucester – Ledbury. A rare instance of animation at a Great Western halt.

B. J. Ashworth

The Lodge Halt, Brymbo, serving a remote local community. Soon after opening, in 1906.

Chetnole Halt on the Dorchester – Yeovil line, in 1964.

Abertafol Halt looking west towards Aberdovey in November 1935. The exposed position of the stopping place is typical of the former Cambrian lines, where whirlwinds were, and are, by no means uncommon. Construction of the platform and shelter would seem to be along conventional lines but of particular interest is the wooden bungalow, on what is obviously railway property. This is thought to have been for the local ganger, accommodation in the area being somewhat scarce.

National Railway Museum

Great Western Railway Halts

A

ABERANGELL

Situated between Cemmes Road and Dinas Mawddwy on the Mawddwy Branch. Provided with a single platform which opened in 1865 but closed from June 1901 to 31st July 1911. Re-opened and finally closed to passengers on 1st January 1931. Parcels traffic reported as dealt with during period of passenger opening. No suffix carried.

ABERCAMLAIS HALT

Situated between Devynock & Sennybridge and Penpont on the former Neath & Brecon line. Opening date uncertain but believed to be sometime in 1870. Single platform provided. Existed as a private stopping place until about February 1930 when the Halt suffix was added.

ABERCWMBOI HALT

see entry for Duffryn Crossing Platform.

Abercwmboi Halt in 1922. (see entry for Duffryn Crossing Platform)

LGRP

Mogul blasting through Abingdon Road Halt on an up train. The humble, slumbering halt, when on a main line at least, could certainly be a place of contrast.
Adrian Vaughan Collection

ABERCWMBOI PLATFORM

see entry for Duffryn Crossing Platform.

ABERDARE COMMERCIAL STREET PLATFORM

South of Aberdare station, on the line to Aberaman. Single platform. Opening date not reported; closed in June 1912.

ABERDARE MILL STREET PLAT-FORM

Situated north of Aberdare Station on the single line leading towards Ysguborwen colliery. Opening date not reported, closed in June 1912.

ABERDERFYN HALT

Situated north of Ponkey Crossing on the single line Ponkey branch from Ruabon. Opened 5th June 1905 and closed to passengers from 22nd March 1915.

ABERDYLAIS

Situated between Clyne Halt and Neath on the main Vale of Neath line. Date of opening not reported. Not believed Halt suffix ever carried.

ABERFFRWD

Sited between Aberystwyth and Devil's Bridge on the narrow gauge Vale of Rheidol Railway. Opened to goods in August 1902 and to passengers from 22nd December 1902. Closed at various times, mainly during the winter months between 1931 and 1945. Further reading; The Vale of Rheidol Light Railway – Wild Swan

ABER JUNCTION HALT

See entry for Beddau Halt. Refer also to entry for Beddau Platform.

ABERTAFOL HALT

Situated between Penhelig Halt and Gogarth Halt on the former Cambrian Railway single line to Pwllheli. Opened 18th March 1935.

ABERTHIN PLATFORM

Between Cowbridge and Trewhyngyll & Maendy Halt on the Taff Vale Railway.

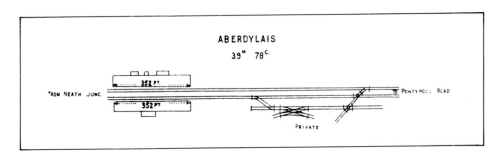

Aber Junction Halt on the former Rhymney Railway. It was opened under another name – see Beddau Halt.

LGRP

Opened 1st May 1905, and it is recorded that parcels were dealt with at the single platform. Temporarily closed from 12th June 1920 and shown in official records for 1928 as still closed. Believed re-opened for a short while after this but finally closed around 1930. Further reading; The Cowbridge Railway – OPC

ABINGDON ROAD HALT
61ᴹ 51ᶜ
(CLOSED)

FROM OXFORD
DOWN MAIN
UP MAIN
TO READING

ABINGDON ROAD HALT

On the Radley to Oxford line. Opened 1st. February 1906 at a cost of £474 – although an entry in official records refers to the provision of six 'motor halts' in the Oxford and Thame district on 30th October 1907. Up and down platforms each 150ft long with a shelter and a path to the public road. Closed in 1925. Note – the name Abingdon Road was also carried by Culham Station before being re-named in 1856. (The other locations referred to at this time were Halts at Horsepath, Garsington Bridge, Iffley, Hinksey and Wolvercote). It is believed the intended name for this stopping place was to have been 'Abingdon Road Bridge Halt' but this was never carried. The halt was closed on 22nd March 1915.

ADMASTON

Situated between Wellington and Walcot on the Shrewsbury and Wellington Joint Railway. Up and down platforms, Halt suffix not carried. Opening date uncertain but known to have been prior to 1881.

ALBERTA PLACE HALT

See next entry.

ALBERTA PLACE PLATFORM

Situated between Penarth Town and Lower Penarth on the Penarth branch of the Taff Vale Railway. Single platform, opened 19th September 1904 and renamed Alberta Place Halt from 1st October 1923. At an unknown date up and down platforms were connected, 'for the convenience of passengers', by a footbridge. Supervision of the halt was exercised by the station master at Penarth.

ALFORD HALT

Between Castle Cary and Keinton Mandeville. Up and down platforms opened 21st July 1905 – prior to opening of the Castle Cary and Langport cut off, and believed never to have been provided with waiting shelters.

ALL STRETTON HALT

Situated between Leebotwood and Church Stretton on the Shrewsbury and Hereford Joint line. Authorised on 12th February 1936 and opened on 29th February of the same year. Provided with up and down platforms 80ft long with footpaths, steps to a road, waiting shelters, name and notice boards, fencing, gates, lighting and drainage. Estimated cost of the work £300. Temporarily closed between 4th January 1943 and 6th May 1946.

Abingdon Road Halt from the road overbridge, looking south in 1919. This Halt was situated 61 miles 51 chains from Paddington but little is known of the place except that it was a regular stopping place for the steam railmotor services Oxford to Princes Risborough, in the period 1908 – 1915. It is believed the shelter was officially a 'Class A' structure, more commonly referred to as a 'Pagoda'.

LGRP

Alford Halt was unusual in that it was provided with a ramp at one end only – at the western extremity there was simply a wooden fence. Access was by pathways to either side, leading to a brick overbridge immediately behind the photographer. Supervision was exercised from nearby Keinton Mandeville.

Lens of Sutton

A close up of the wooden All Stretton shelter, on the up platform. Both platform buildings (see opposite) appear to have been identical. The attempt at a simple form of bargeboard design is of interest whilst the practice of using old sleepers wherever possible is readily visible.

National Railway Museum

Rear detail of the All Stretton shelter, and what would appear to be old GW 2 hole sleepers, as the main supports.

National Railway Museum

Exeter train at Alphington.

Alphington Halt looking towards Christow on the Teign Valley line Public access was via a ramp, and wooden slats helped to avoid slipping in wet or icy conditions. Cleaning etc. was undertaken from Exeter St. Thomas.

Lens of Sutton

All Stretton Halt looking north, with the cheapness of construction common to so many halts readily apparent. 6th November 1935.

National Railway Museum

ALLTDDU HALT

Situated between Tregaron and Strata Florida on the Aberystwyth branch. Single platform authorised on 3rd October 1935 at an estimated cost of £170. Opened to traffic on 23rd September 1935.

ALPHINGTON HALT

Between Exeter St.Thomas and Ide Halt, opened on 2nd April 1928. Provided with a single wooden platform 100 ft. long, having a corrugated shelter with a flat roof. Further reading; The Teign Valley Line – Oakwood Press.

ALVERLEY HALT

See next entry.

ALVERLEY COLLIERY HALT

Single platform between Hampton Loade and Highley on the west side of the line. Opening date is uncertain with some sources quoting 1915 and others as late as 22nd December 1944. Originally unadvertised in timetables and used by colliery workers. Sometimes referred to as Alverley Colliery Sidings. At an undisclosed date, and possibly not until the BR era, the name was altered to Alverley Halt and the stopping place began to appear in the passenger timetables.

GREAT WESTERN RAILWAY.

On Monday, April 2nd, 1928,

A NEW HALT

WILL BE OPENED AT

ALPHINGTON

SITUATE BETWEEN

EXETER (ST. THOMAS) AND IDE HALT.

TRAIN SERVICE. Week-days only.

		M	M	M	M	M	M	M	M		M	M
		a.m.	a.m.	a.m.	p.m.	p.m.	p.m.	p.m.	p.m.		p.m.	p.m.
Exeter St. David's	dep.	7 0	9 30	10 58	12 55	2 45	..	..	5 43	..	8 45	9S40
Exeter St. Thomas	..	7 4	9 34	11 3	12 58	2 50	..	..	5 47	..	8 49	9S44
ALPHINGTON HALT	..	7 8	9 38	11 7	1 [illegible]	2 54	..	..	5 51	..	8 53	9S48
Ide Halt	..	7 12	9 43	11 11	1 7	2 59	..	..	5 55	..	8 57	9S52
Longdown	..	7 21	9 52	11 20	1 16	3 8	..	..	6 4	..	9 6	10S 1
Dunsford Halt	..	7 25	9 56	11 24	1 20	3 12	..	..	6 8	..	9 10	10S 5
Christow	..	7 31	10 2	11 30	1 30	3 17	4 13	..	6 17	..	9 20	10S11
Ashton	..	7 36	10 7	11 35	1 35		4 18	..	6 22	..	9 25	10S16
Trusham	..	7 44	10 15	11 43	1 43	..	4 26	..	6 30	..	9 33	10S24
Chudleigh	..	7 50	10 21	11 49	1 49	..	4 32	5 23	6 36	..	9 39	10S30
Chudleigh Knighton Halt	..	7 54	10 25	11 53	1 53	..	4 36	5 27	6 40	..	9 43	10S34
Heathfield	arr.	7 58	10 29	11 57	1 57	..	4 40	5 31	6 44	..	9 47	10S38
Heathfield	dep.	8 5	10 35	12 56	2M10	..	5 35	5 35	7 40	..	9W50	..
Bovey	arr.	8 14	10 43	1 3	2M15	..	5 44	5 44	7 47	..	9W57	..
Moretonhampstead	..	8 34	11 5	1 25	3T 55	..	6 5	6 5	8 9	..	10W19	..
Heathfield	dep.	8 20	10 50	12 0	2 3	..	4 45	..	6 49	..	9 50	..
Newton Abbot	arr.	8 30	11 0	12 10	2 13	..	4 55	..	7 0	..	10 0	..

		a.m.	a.m.	p.m.		p.m.	p.m.	p.m.		p.m.		p.m.
Newton Abbot	dep	7 55	10 25	12 46	..	3 15	..	5 25	..	7 30	..	9S40
Heathfield	arr.	8 5	10 35	12 56	..	3 25	..	5 35	..	7 40	..	9S50
Moretonhampstead	dep.	7 55	10 25	11‡35	..	1 40	4 20	4 20	..	6 25	..	8S20
Bovey	..	8 13	10 43	11‡53	..	2M30	4 38	4 38	..	6 42	..	8S36
Heathfield	arr.	8 20	10 50	12 0	..	2M36	4 45	4 45	..	6 49	..	8S42
		M	M	M		M	M	M		M		M
Heathfield	dep	8 23	10 53	1 0	..	3 30	5 10	5 40	..	7 45	..	10S45
Chudleigh Knighton Halt	..	8 28	10 58	1 5	..	3 35	5 15	5 45	..	7 50	..	10S50
Chudleigh	..	8 32	11 2	1 9	..	3 39	5 18	5 49	..	7 54	..	10S54
Trusham	..	8 38	11 8	1 15	..	3 45		5 55	..	8 0	..	11S 0
Ashton	..	8 44	11 14	1 21	..	3 51	..	6 1	..	8 7	..	11S 6
Christow	..	8 50	11U31	1 27	..	3 57	..	6X15	..	8 13	..	11S12
Dunsford Halt	..	8 57	11 38	1 34	..	4 4	..	6 22	..	8 20	..	11S19
Longdown	..	9 0	11 41	1 37	..	4 7	..	6 25	..	8 23	..	11S22
Ide Halt	..	9 7	11 48	1 44	..	4 14	..	6 32	..	8 30	..	11S29
ALPHINGTON HALT	..	9 11	11 52	1 48	..	4 18	..	6 36	..	8 34	..	11S33
Exeter St. Thomas	..	9 16	11 57	1 52	..	4 26	..	6 40	..	8 38	..	11S40
Exeter St. David's	arr.	9 19	12 0	1 58	..	4 29	..	6 43	..	8 41	..	11S43

M—Rail Motor Car, one class only. S—Saturdays only. T—Heathfield depart 3 25 p.m. U—Arrives Christow 11.19 a.m. W—Saturdays only until April 28th, daily commencing April 30th. X—Arrives Christow 6 6 p.m. ‡—a.m.

Tickets should be obtained from the Guard on the train.

The Third Class Single Fares from ALPHINGTON HALT will be as under:—

	s.	d.		s.	d.
Ashton (Devon)	1	2	Heathfield	2	0
Christow		11½	Ide Halt		2½
Chudleigh	1	8	Longdown		6
Chudleigh Knighton Halt	1	9	Newton Abbot (via Heathfield)	2	6
Dawlish (via St. Thomas)	1	7	Teigngrace	2	3
Dunsford Halt		8½	Teignmouth (via Newton Abbot)	2	8
Exeter, St. David's		3	Trusham	1	6
" St. Thomas		2½			

CHEAP THIRD-CLASS RETURN TICKETS will be issued each week-day by ANY TRAIN—

To EXETER (St. David's) s. d. 3 | To NEWTON ABBOT (via Heathfield) s. 2 d. 5

These Tickets will be available for return on day of Outward Journey by any train.

Parcels and Goods traffic will not be dealt with at the Halt.

Paddington, March, 1928.

FELIX J. C. POLE, General Manager.

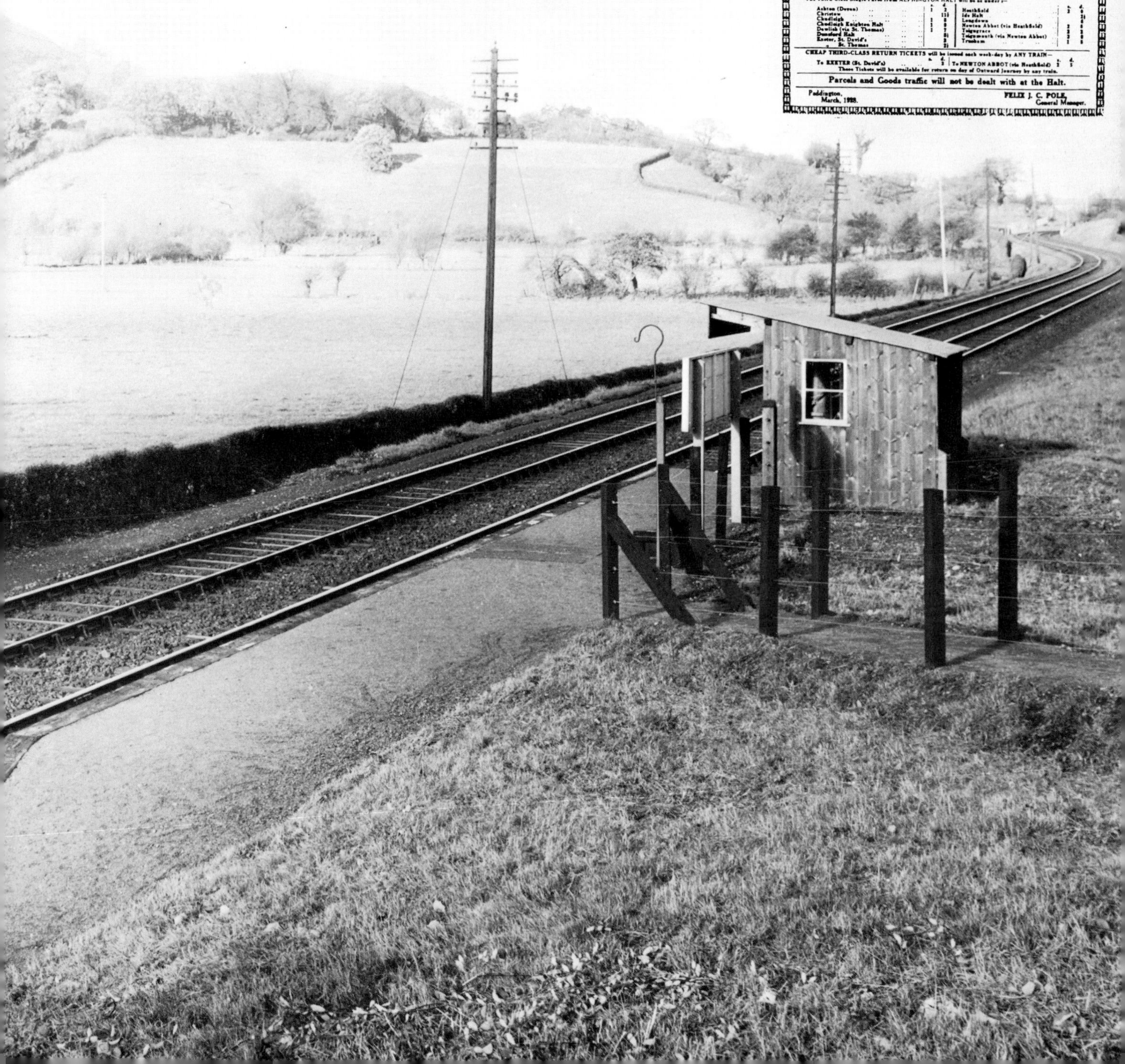

Appleford Halt in BR days with No. 6122 entering the stopping place, at the head of a Didcot-bound stopping service. Notice the steps leading up to the roadbridge, affording convenient access between the two platforms.

Lawrence Waters

Activity at 'Ashton Gate Halte, Bristol'.

Brian Hilton Collection

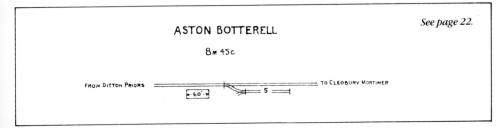

ASTON BOTTERELL

See page 22.

8m 45c

FROM DITTON PRIORS — TO CLEOBURY MORTIMER

ALVERLEY COLLIERY SIDINGS

See previous entry.

AMMANFORD COLLIERY HALT

Single platform, between Ammanford and Glanaman. Opened 1st May 1905. This was an unstaffed stopping place at which trains would call during daylight hours only. A solitary brick/corrugated iron waiting shelter was provided, tickets being obtained from the signal box at the end of the platform.

APPLEFORD HALT

Sited between Didcot and Culham. Authorised on 25th May 1933 and consisting of timber up and down platforms (200ft by 8ft), standard pagoda shelters, name boards, gates, steps and electric lighting — total cost £588. Opened on 11th September 1933 and unstaffed, tickets were obtained from the Post Office in Appleford. Access between the two platforms was by means of wooden steps to the nearby road overbridge. For accounting purposes receipts from Appleford Halt were included with nearby Culham Station. Construction of this halt involved refixing a platelayers hut to a new site further down the line. (A station with the name Appleford is also spoken of in early GWR timetables in the period up to 1849)

ARDDLEEN HALT

Single platform between Four Crosses and Pool Quay on the Whitchurch and Aberystwyth line of the Cambrian Railway. Opening date uncertain and it is not believed that any suffix was ever carried.

ASHTON GATE

See entry for Ashton Gate Platform.

ASHTON GATE PLATFORM

Situated between Parson Street and Clifton Bridge on the Portishead branch. Up and down platforms reported as 'opened' on 1st October 1910. A further entry refers to a re-opening on 23rd May 1926. Officially renamed Ashton Gate c.August 1928 although nameboard retained 'platform' suffix. Its main use believed to have been in connection with football matches.

Ashton Gate, in BR days, but otherwise basically unaltered from the time of opening. The view is taken in the down direction towards Portishead. On the right the line leads towards Wapping Wharf and Canon's Marsh.

LGRP

Arddleen, between Four Crosses and Pool Quay. Notice there is no 'Halt' suffix.

Lens of Sutton

Aston Botterell siding on the former C.M & D.P Railway. The primitive facilities were hardly likely to encourage passenger traffic. Despite such limited resources parcels were handled 'as required.'

Roger Carpenter Collection

ASTON BOTTERELL SIDING

Situated between Stottesdon and Burwater on the Cleobury Mortimer and Ditton Priors Railway. Opened 21st November 1908 it had a single low height platform with no shelter but parcels traffic is recorded as having been dealt with. Closed to passengers along with the C.M.& D.P. Railway on 25 September 1938.

ASTON CANTLOW HALT

Single platform between Bearley and Great Alne on the Alcester branch. Authorised on 1st June 1922 at an estimated cost of £327. Opened 18th December 1922. Closed 25th September 1939.

ASTWOOD HALT

Between Worcester and Fernhill Heath. Authorised by the GWR on 19th December 1935. it consisted of up and down platforms, paths and steps to road, shelters, name and notice boards, fencing, gates and lighting. Estimated cost of £527. Opened 18th May 1936. Closed 25th September 1939.

Ashton Gate. Viewed from the other side the solid platforms and commodious footbridge are an reminder of busier times in the past.

Lens of Sutton

Avoncliff seen from the Kennet and Avon canal overbrige, after the platforms had been raised to standard height. Passenger access between the two platforms was via the cinder and ballast pathway. The space between the running lines is a legacy of the broad gauge on this former 'Wilts Somerset and Weymouth' line. Nearby was a private siding operated by Messrs. Randell and Saunders.

Lens of Sutton

AVINGTON

Unadvertised stopping place on military line north of Winchester Chesil (D.N & S.) line. In use by 20th October 1918 and served by a shuttle service from Winchester. Facilities at this sprawling Army depot are unconfirmed and there may have been more than one stopping place within the camp. Out of use by November 1920. Further reading, The Didcot, Newbury & Southampton Railway. Wild Swan.

AVONCLIFF HALT

Situated between Bradford-on-Avon and Freshford. A letter sent by the GWR to the Board of Trade on 15th June 1906 requested provisional sanction for a stopping place for 'rail motor cars'. This was granted and the halt opened for public services on 9th July 1906. A further letter from the GWR was sent to the Board of Trade on 12th July 1906 stating the work as ready for inspection, and Colonel Yorke attended on 24th August 1906. He reported as follows:

.....I have inspected the new motor halte at Avoncliff, on the Bradford branch of the Great Western Railway. The Halte comprises two platforms each 100ft long, 7ft wide and 14 inches above rail level. There are no shelters but the platforms are provided with lamps and name boards. The Halte is suitable only for and should be used only by special rail motor cars fitted with folding steps. At a later time standard height platforms of the same length were provided, together with wooden shelters.

Aynho Park Platform on the 'new line,' facing Princes' Risborough. The designation 'Platform' does not appear on the nameboard and likewise does not seem to have been used in the public timetable.

Mowat Collection

Avoncliff Halt with the earlier Kennet and Avon Canal passing overhead by means of the Avoncliff Aqueduct at the end of the platform. From a study of photographs it would appear there were several design options open to the GWR with regard to the type of shelter used at halts and platforms. Those here, though of the smallest timber variant, were obviously better than having no protection at all!

Lens of Sutton

AVONCLIFF HALT

STONE FIRMS SIDING

FROM BRISTOL
UP MAIN LINE
DOWN MAIN LINE
TO PADDINGTON
100 FT
100 FT

AVONCLIFF SIDING
S.B.

AYNHO PARK PLATFORM

Situated between Ardley and Kings Sutton on the Ashendon and Aynho line. Up and down platforms, opened on 1st July 1910.

Brimscombe Bridge – see later, pages 38 and 39 – closer to the road overbridge the position of the opposite platform is readily apparent, as is the access path leading down from the roadway alongside the line.

LGRP

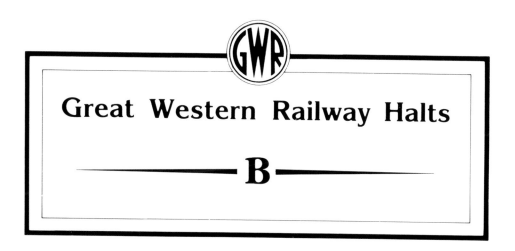

Great Western Railway Halts
— B —

BACKNEY HALT

Situated between Ross-on-Wye and Fawley. Single platform authorised on 23rd March 1933 at an estimated cost of £250. Opened 17th July 1933.

BACTON

Single platform situated between Abbeydore and Vowchurch. Opening date uncertain; had originally been a conditional stopping place in the days of the independent Golden Valley railway. At that time it was referred to as Bacton Road. A period of temporary closure occurred during the First World War and final closure to passengers came on 15th December 1941. Parcels traffic was reportedly handled.

BAGLAN SANDS HALT

Situated between Aberavon and Briton Ferry. Up and down platforms opened 1st May 1933. Closed 25th September 1939.

BALA LAKE HALT

Single platform between Llandderfel and Llanuwchllyn. Opened 5th February 1934. The stopping place was on the same site as the original Bala station closed in 1883. A GWR document of 23rd January 1934 refers as follows: *A new halt at Bala Lake which is situated 2 miles 22 chains from Llangower Halt and 51 chains from Bala Junction Station will be completed on Monday February 5th. It is not the intention that the halt should be used for regular services (to commence with), but only for Excursion trains on Sundays and special occasions.*

BALDWIN'S HALT

Situated between Danygraig and Jersey Marine. Up and down platforms opened to public services from 24th November 1924, although the halt had existed prior to this (from July 1911 it is believed) as an unadvertised stopping place. A note in the records on 25th October 1912 refers to the provision of a 'standard shelter' on the down platform at an estimated cost of £50. Parcels traffic was handled. Closed 11th September 1939.

BAPTIST END HALT

Put up between Windmill End and Blowers Green. Up and down platforms, opened 21st August 1905. On 22nd October 1923 a suggestion was received from a member of staff as to improved lighting; this was not proceeded with. Further reading – Railways of the Black Country. Uralia Press.

BARGOED COLLIERY HALT

Single platform existing as an unadvertised stopping place on the Brecon & Merthyr line between Gwaelodywaen Colliery and Aberbargoed. Official records report the stopping place was authorised on 26th July 1934 at a cost of £145. (An unconfirmed source states that the halt was in use as early as September 1926). Not believed a nameboard was carried.

BARTON STACEY HALT

Situated between Sutton Scotney and Whitchurch (Hants). Platform on east side of the single line, used by workmen building a nearby army camp of same name. Believed to have opened during the summer of 1940/41, served by a morning and evening shuttle service operating between Winchester and Whitchurch Great Western stations. A brief life, and an unusual closure. A

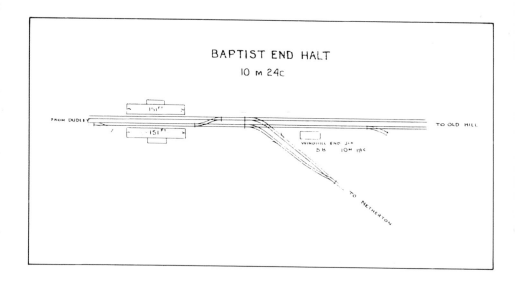

BAPTIST END HALT
10 m 24c

Beanacre Halt, looking in the up direction towards Chippenham. This was one of the few main line halts to retain its low platform.

LGRP

Bilson Halt on the Forest of Dean branch, viewed north towards Bilson loop and Cinderford. The close proximity of Cinderford itself has led to the name 'Bilson Cinderford' being proclaimed on the noticeboard. In the background is Letcher Bridge.

BEAVERS HILL HALT

21M· 1°

FROM PEMBROKE   O.G.F.   TO WHITLAND

130FT

runaway steamroller ran into it, the damage such that it was abandoned, in December 1941. Further reading – the Didcot, Newbury & Southampton Rly, Wild Swan.

BATHFORD HALT

The halt lay between Box and Bathampton and was authorised on 4th October 1928 with up and down platforms 250ft by 8ft with shelters, footpaths, steps, retaining walls and lighting. Electric lighting with time switches was later substituted. Estimated cost of construction reported as £164. Opened 18th March 1929. No staff provided but tickets available from a local agent. Supervision exercised from Bathampton.

BEACONSFIELD GOLF LINKS HALT

Between Gerrards Cross and Beaconsfield on the GW – GC joint line. Originally a private stopping place for golfers under the name Beaconsfield Golf Platform, from 2nd April 1906 until 1st January 1915. Opened to public services from 1st January 1915 and renamed Seer Green on 16th December 1918. Up and down platforms with standard pagoda shelters provided and passenger access via pathways leading down to the public road.

BEANACRE HALT

Situated between Chippenham and Melksham. Up and down platforms, opened 29th October 1905.

BEAUFORT

Situated beyond Ebbw Vale serving a colliery. In use as a private stopping place by 1886.

BEAUPRE

Proposal from an influential resident for a platform between Cowbridge and St. Hilary Platform. Rejected by the Taff Vale Railway in January 1906. Further reading – The Cowbridge Railway, OPC.

BEAVERS HILL HALT

Opened 1st May 1905, between Manorbier and Lampney. Temporary closure from 21st October 1914 to 1st December 1923. Single timber platform, 130ft long, in later years devoid of any shelter. Further reading – The Pembroke & Tenby Railway, Oakwood Press.

BEDDAU HALT

Up and down platforms, opened April 1908 between Caerphilly and Llanbradach on the Rhymney Railway. Sometimes incorrectly referred to as Beda Halt. Renamed Aber Junction Halt on 17th June 1926. See also entry for Beddau Platform.

BEDDAU PLATFORM

See also entry for Beddau Halt. Single platform between Llantwit and Cross Inn on the Taff Vale Railway. Opened July 1910, renamed Beddau Halt on 1st October 1923.

BEDLINOG COLLIERY JUNCTION

Unadvertised stopping place situated between Bedlinog and Nantyffyn. In use by July 1897 and believed closed in November 1915. Provided with staggered platforms. In use again from an unknown date prior to 1938.

BEDLINOG WORKMENS PLATFORM

Unadvertised stopping place on the branch from Bedlinog Colliery Junction. In use sometime after 1915 and closed by 1938.

BERWIG HALT

Situated between Vicarage Crossing Halt and Croes Newydd Fork. Opened 1st May 1905 with parcels traffic recorded as handled. Temporary closure from 1st January 1917 to 2nd April 1917, finally closed to all traffic from 1st January 1931. Single wooden platform provided on the up side of the line with a wooden booking office and corrugated shelter. The Halt served the villages of Gwynfryn and Minerva. In charge of the stopping place was a Grade 1 Porter who resided in a GWR owned cottage nearby. Supervision was exercised from Coed Poeth.

BERW ROAD HALT
See Berw Road Platform

BERW ROAD PLATFORM

Taff Vale Railway, situated between Pontypridd and Clifynydd. Opened 17th October 1904. Temporary closure from 1st July 1906 to July 1908 and renamed Berw Road Halt from 2nd October 1922. Closed to passengers 12th September 1932.

BERWYN

Situated on the single line between Glyndyfrdwy and Llangollen. Originally opened as a station, date of downgrading not reported.

BEULAH HALT

Between Puncheston and Letterston. Single platform opened 24th September 1928. Closed 25th October 1937.

BILSON HALT

Between Newnham and Cinderford. Single platform opened 3rd August 1907. Temporary closure between 6th April 1908 and 2nd April 1917. At varying times in use as an unadvertised miners' stopping place.

BILSON ROAD PLATFORM

Single platform 80 feet in length with a shelter 18 feet by 6 feet, on the line between Laymoor Junction and Cinderford Junction. Opened 1st September 1876. Further reading – The Severn & Wye Railway Vol. 2. Wild Swan.

Birches and Bilbrook. A close up of the shelter, clearly of cheap manufacture and somewhat crude in construction. It has not been possible to determine with certainty why some stopping places were afforded a 'standard' building and others were not.

Lens of Sutton

BE

'Berwig Station and Crossing'. If railways were in
harmony with their surroundings then with stopping places this quality was enhanced even further.
There is nothing in this scene that lacks scale, pro-
portion, or the proper contrast, despite differences
in material and widely separate generations of
building and land use.

Collection Brian Hilton

VIG-Station & Crossing

Birches & Bilbrook Halt revealing the staggered arrangement of the platforms. Access between them was over a road overbridge.

Lens of Sutton

Birchgrove Halt in BR days, after the line had been singled. The 1935 platform extensions, which more than doubled the length available, are apparent

Lens of Sutton

An up passenger train with a Churchward 4-4-0 at its head, working hard on the climb through Bittaford platform. Notice the original condition of the platforms, which are of timber construction.

Lens of Sutton

Taken some time after the previous view, by now the platforms have been rebuilt with masonry. The nameboard fails to give the full name, a relatively common occurence, which in the case of a number of locations in the past has given rise to confusion. Which were 'Halts' and which 'Platforms', and vice versa?

Lens of Sutton

Black Dog Halt on the Calne branch from Chippenham, originally opened as a private stopping place and siding for Lord Lansdowne.

D. Thompson

BIRCHES AND BILBROOK HALT

Halt between Dunstall Park and Codsall. Authorised on 26th April 1934 at an estimated cost of £268 for staggered up and down platforms. Actual cost of facilities reported as £267. 19s. Opened 30th April 1934. At an unreported date renamed 'Bilbrook Halt'

BIRCHGROVE HALT

Situated between Heath Low Level and Whitchurch. Authorised on 20th March 1929 at an estimated cost of £391 and originally to have been called 'Phoenix Bridge, Caerphilly'. Opened 10th June 1929. Improvements authorised on 30th May 1935 consequent upon the running of longer trains on the Rhiwbina branch, an extension of the down platform from 196 feet to 400 feet and up platform from 267 feet to 400 feet. Also electric lighting and additional nameboards, cost reported as £255.

BISHOPSTEIGNTON HALT

1923 entry in GWR Suggestions Committee Minutes for a Halt between Teignmouth and Newton Abbot to meet road competition; 'Not proceeded with'.

BITTAFORD PLATFORM

Between Wrangaton and Ivybridge. Up and down platforms opened 18th November 1907. Parcels traffic handled.

BLACK DOG HALT

Private stopping place between Stanley Bridge Halt and Calne in use c.1863 on land belonging to the estate of Lord Lansdowne. At that time was referred to as Black Dog siding, a platform was in use from at least 1873. A surviving letter agreement 20th April 1875 gives details of the original staffing arrangements at the siding: 'A man to be appointed by the Great Western Railway to take charge of the siding – light the lamps – give signals – check tickets (when necessary) book parcels and do all the work the GW may require of him and in addition he should look after Lord Landsdowne's stores, coals – and any other work that may be required of him at the station consistent with his first duty to the company – and that he shall be paid 20 shillings per week

besides being found a house and coal by Lord Lansdowne. That in addition to finding the house and coal Lord Lansdowne will pay a sum of 8 shillings weekly towards the man's pay – the GW paying the difference of 12 shillings and finding clothes and the admin stores for working the station – signals, etc. Six months notice given at any time to be sufficient to terminate this agreement.' On 1st May 1895. the following was reported: ' Erection of booking office, new corrugated iron lamp hut and conversion of existing lamp hut into lock up at Black Dog Siding. Also removal of signal cabin and signal, the siding being worked by Annetts Key. £97.'

BLACK LION CROSSING HALT

Originally opened on 1st January 1904 as a private platform for use by miners and unadvertised in public timetables. Between Dare Junction and Cwmaman Colliery. GWR records of 3rd May 1905 refer to the conversion of the stopping place to a public platform although no date for this is given.

Blaisdon halt with the alternative style of corrugated shelter often employed at minor stopping places. It would appear this type of hut had several other uses, at different locations, including a permanent way store, large lamp hut and paraffin store.

Lens of Sutton

Bledlow Bridge Halt on the Watlington Branch, viewed towards Princes Risborough in 1919. Unusually for the period there is a surfeit of weeds, a contrast to the customary tidy appearance of the railway at this time. A place of similar name, Bledlow Station, was provided on the nearby Thame branch.

LGRP

Closed from 1st January 1906. Reported reopened from 22nd September 1924 although this is contradicted by a 1928 report, which states that the location was 'at present closed'.

BLACKPOLE HALT

Unadvertised stopping place for an Ordnance Factory between Fernhill Heath and Astwood Halt, provided with up and down platforms. In use between 1917 and 1920 and again from 1940 to 1946. Not confirmed if Halt suffix was carried.

BLACK ROCK HALT

On the south side of the single line between Portmadoc and Criccieth. Authorised on 12th April 1923 with shelter, nameboard and access path from the nearby beach at a cost of £242 to the Engineering Department and £15 to the Signal department. Originally to have been called Blackpole Halt. Opened 9th July 1923. Further reading – Scenes From The Past No.4, The Cambrian Coast Rly, Foxline.

BLAENDARE ROAD HALT

Authorised on 6th October 1927, sited between Pontypool (Crane Street) and Panteg. Slightly staggered up and down platforms, shelters and footpath to road. Estimated cost £458. Opened 30th April 1928. Nameboards proclaimed 'Pontypool Blaendare Road.'

BLAENPLWYF HALT

Situated between Lampeter and Aberayron. Single platform opened 12th May 1911.

MILL LANE BOX. G.W.R.

Box (Mill Lane) Halt with the original timber platforms just visible.

Lens of Sutton

A later view of the stopping place with nameboards proclaiming simply 'Mill Lane'. Notice also the replacement concrete platforms, though the corrugated shelters appear to be original.

D. Thompson

BLAISDON HALT

Between Grange Court and Longhope. Single platform opened 4th November 1929.

BLEDLOW BRIDGE HALT

Situated between Princes Risborough and Chinnor. Opened 1st September 1906 and unstaffed. Single 70 ft. low platform on up side of the line having a simple wooden shelter. Access via a gateway and steps leading down to road level. Traffic receipts included with Watlington Station although supervision exercised from Chinnor.

BOLHAM HALT

Opened 23rd April 1928 under the control of Tiverton. Single platform between Bampton and Tiverton, with corrugated iron shelter having a flat roof. The platform was just one and a half coaches in length with access from a set of steps leading down to a nearby road under-bridge. Further reading

– The Exe Valley Railway, Kingfisher.

BONWM HALT

Single platform with timber shelter, opened 21st September 1935. Official records of 3rd October 1935 report the cost of construction to have been £141. Between Carrog and Corwen.

```
┌─────────────────────────────────────────────────┐
│           BLEDLOW BRIDGE HALT                   │
│                 1ᴹ 43ᶜ                          │
│                                                 │
│  FROM WATLINGTON              TO PRINCES RISBOROUGH │
│              ┊········ 70 FT ········┊           │
└─────────────────────────────────────────────────┘
```

Boxford on the former Lambourn Valley line from Newbury, which was designated a Halt by the GWR despite being staffed and having a goods siding. 'Halt' was never carried on the nameboards and supervision was exercised from Lambourn. On the platform the nearest building is thought to date from independent days. At the time of writing it still survives as a bus shelter, on the nearby road.

LGRP

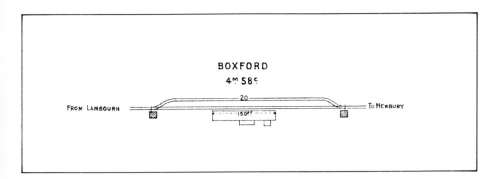

BOXFORD

4ᵐ 58ᶜ

FROM LAMBOURN — 20 — To NEWBURY

150ᶠᵗ

BOUGHTON HALT

Situated between Henwick and Bransford Road. 'Up' and 'down' platforms opened 31st March 1924.

BOURNVILLE HALT (MONMOUTH)

Situated between Abertillery and Blaina. Up and down platforms opened to public services on 30th September 1933. Had previously existed as the unadvertised Tylers Arms Platform. In use in latter guise by 3rd June 1915.

BOWBRIDGE CROSSING HALT

Between Brimscombe and Stroud. Up and down platforms opened 1st May 1905.

BOXFORD

Located between Lambourn and Newbury. Opened 4th April 1898 originally having a single low platform on the west side of the line, for the rolling stock of the independent Lambourn Valley Railway. Rebuilt after acquisition by the GWR to standard height. The Halt suffix never referred to in time-tables or station notices. Further reading – The Lambourn Branch, Pub. Wild Swan.

BOX (MILL LANE) HALT

Situated between Corsham and Box and authorised on 28th November 1929. Opened on 31st March 1930 with up and down platforms 250 ft. long by 8 ft. wide with waiting shelters, booking office at street level, footpaths, nameboards, fencing

and drainage. Electric lighting also provided. Total estimated cost £800. The stopping place was located between Middle Hill and Box tunnels. A member of staff was provided for much of the day to deal with passengers, parcels and miscellaneous traffic whilst outside working hours the guard of trains calling at the Halt would collect tickets, note the number of passengers joining, as well as extinguish the lights on departure of the last train. A census reveals the levels of traffic in 1938 and 1946 as follows:

1938 January to October: 13,824 passengers booked, £993 passenger receipts, £7 parcels.
1946 January to October: 13,989 passengers booked, £1409 passenger receipts, £13 parcels.

BRADFORD PEVERELL AND STRATTON HALT

Located between Grimstone & Frampton and Dorchester. Authorised on 23rd March 1933 with staggered up and down platforms 150 ft. long, shelters, footpath to road, gates and lighting. Estimated cost £575. Opened 22nd May 1933. Further reading – The Bath to Weymouth Line, Oakwood.

Bolham Halt looking north towards Bampton on the Exe Valley line. It was unusual in that (it is believed) a concrete platform was provided from the outset.

Lens of Sutton

Bowbridge Crossing Halt in the Stroud Valley on the route of the original steam railmotor service. The view was taken some years after the stopping place had opened; it depicts standard height platforms which had replaced the original ground level arrangements.

LGRP

'Bradford Peverell and Stratton Halt' on 28th August 1964. Halts frequently boasted grand names, an attempt (often vain) to gather in traffic from as wide an area as possible.

Brian Hilton Collection

BRAMPFORD SPEKE HALT

Originally a station, opened 1st August 1884 between Thorverton and Stoke Canon. Temporary closure from 1st January 1917 to 1st January 1919. Renamed and rendered unstaffed from 1st October 1923 from which date goods traffic was no longer dealt with. Parcels were handled although the original station facilities were no longer available – a poor substitute being an open corrugated hut. Cleaning and maintenance exercised from Stoke Canon. Further reading – The Exe Valley Railway, Kingfisher.

BREAN ROAD HALT

Situated between Bleadon and Brent Knoll. Authorised on 25th April 1929 with up and down platforms 400 ft. by 8 ft, shelters, booking office, road and footpath approaches, steps, fencing and paraffin vapour lighting. Estimated cost of £1277 but actual cost was £1487. Originally to have been called Brean Bridge Halt. Opened 17th June 1929. Milk and general produce traffic, which for accountancy purposes was dealt with by Brent Knoll station, although Highbridge was the supervising station.

BRENTHAM HALT

Opened 1st May 1911 at an estimated cost of £980 and situated between Park Royal and Greenford. Provided with up and down platforms 400 ft. by 12 ft, porch, booking office and corrugated shelters recovered from the former Twyford Abbey Halt. Referred in official publications as 'Brentham (for North Ealing).' For accountancy purposes included with either Greenford or Southall. The GWR Suggestions Committee meeting of 11th February 1924 contains the entry: 'Timebill boards at Brentham

Halt to be removed from their present position and placed under a lamp where they can be read by passengers after dark.' The un-named author of this suggestion was awarded a gratuity of 10/6d. Closed 30th June 1947 – see also entry for Twyford Abbey Halt.

BRIMLEY HALT

Situated on the east side of the single line between Heathfield and Bovey. Opened 21st May 1928 under the control of the Bovey station master.

BRIMSCOMBE BRIDGE HALT

Situated between Brimscombe and Stroud. Staggered up and down platforms, opened 1st February 1904. Approval given for electric lighting on 9th February 1939 at a cost of £90. A surviving inventory of furniture for August 1904 provides details of the original facilities:

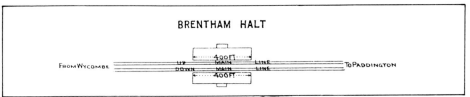

BRENTHAM HALT

Stool	2s 6d
1 Ticket Box 18″x18″x18″	10s
1 Oil Lamp	2s 6d
1 Cabin Box 12′x8′6″x9′ wood	£10 0s 0d
2 Boards No.7	£2 8s 0d
1 Board No.4	14s 6d
1 Board – Halt	17s 0d
2 Crossing Nameboards 11′6″x1′6″	£2 10s 0d
1 Ink Well	5d
1 Shovel	1s 6d
1 Shelter, galvanised 20′x8′x10′	£20 0s 0d

BRITISH RHONDDA HALT

Between Hirwaun and Glyn Neath, a single platform serving down line only, opened 27th August 1906. Closed 1st May 1911.

Despite the single platform it was served by trains in both directions with those from Swansea reversing over a nearby trailing crossover. (Superseded by Pontwalby Halt which opened 1st May 1911, less than a quarter of a mile from original site and using material salvaged from British Rhondda Halt.) Not surprisingly, bearing in mind the unusual arrangements at this Halt, the location came in for careful study by the Board of Trade. The GWR wrote on 12th July 1906; 'It will be observed that it is proposed to provide a platform on the down side of the line only, it being the intention for cars on the up road to run ahead and back over the cross over road which will be fitted with facing point locks and locking bars'.....

On 31st August 1906 Colonel Yorke attended the site and reported as follows:

Brimscombe Bridge Halt was another of those on the route of the original railmotor service although here in much altered form. The pagoda shelter is of the recognised standard design although the office alongside is of more unusual construction.

National Railway Museum

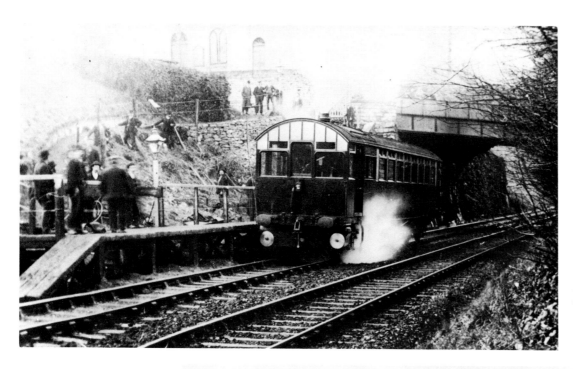

Brimscombe Bridge in earlier guise. Compare with view opposite.

Brean Road Halt viewed towards Bristol. Notice the differing design of shelter on the up and down platforms. On the extreme right is a part view of a concrete post signal, unusually placed to the rear of the platform.

LGRP

Brimscombe Bridge. The Halt was provided with staggered platforms, each linked by a pathway leading from the overbridge. This view shows the up side in 1932.

LGRP

'.....I have inspected the new stopping place for rail motor cars which has been provided at British Rhondda between Glyn Neath and Hirwaun on the Great Western Railway. The line is double but the stopping place consists of a single platform alongside the down line only, the intention being that motor cars on the up road should back over the cross over road between the up and down lines and so reach the platform, it not being intended at present to extend the motor car service between Glyn Neath and British Rhondda beyond the latter place. The platform is 100 ft. long, 7 ft. wide and 3 ft. high. It is provided with a shelter, name board and lamps. The points of the cross over road, which have been fitted with facing point locks are worked from the existing signal box ... and correctly interlocked. The arrangement of a single platform for a double line is somewhat unusual, but having regard to the nature of the traffic I do not think that it need be objected to in this instance, I therefore recommend.....'
Presumably Colonel Yorke had forgotten the original one sided stations on the GWR main line, such as Reading?

BRITANNIA HALT

See entry for Kingswear Level Crossing.

BROAD MARSTON HALT

Between Honeybourne and Long Marston. Up and down platforms opened 17th October 1904. Closed 14th July 1916.

BROADSANDS HALT

Two miles south of Paignton station on Kingswear branch. Single platform authorised on 24th April 1928 with foot-

The single platform at Brimley Halt, between Heathfield and Bovey; a classic example of the GWR's attempts to attract patronage from wherever possible.
Lens of Sutton

Bryngwyn Halt on the former Cambrian system, seen here with replacement concrete fittings. The shelter appears to be formed of a corrugated asbestos type material and is yet another variant from the 'standard' fittings once used. Notice in this view the suffix 'Halt' does not appear.
Lens of Sutton

Bryngwyn from the rear, with the necessary supports (due to the embankment) visible, as is the nameboard, this time stating 'Bryngwyn Halt.' There would also appear to be a variety of lamps in use, both oil and tilley type.
Lens of Sutton

path, steps to road and lighting. Estimated cost of £657. Reported in use for excursion traffic only between 9th July 1928 and 23rd September 1929, although this may be open to doubt. Further reading – The Newton Abbot to Kingswear Railway, Oakwood.

BROCKMOOR HALT

Between Brettell Lane and Himley. Up and down platforms opened 11th May 1925. Closed 31st October 1932.

BROCKWEIR HALT

Situated between Tintern and St. Briavels. Opened 19th August 1929. Single sleeper platform with a cinder surface and having a corrugated waiting shelter with a curved roof. Public access via a path leading up to the road. Further reading – The Wye Valley Railway. Pub. Oakwood.

BROMHAM & ROWDE HALT

Single platform between Devizes and Seend, authorised on 6th May 1908. Opened 22nd February 1909 with waiting shed, milk stage, and lamp hut. Parcels dealt with along with milk, timber and sugar beet. A goods loop of 15 wagons capacity was also opened at the same time and a corrugated iron goods office was also provided. On the same date a private siding was opened. Passengers joining trains here would have tickets issued to them by the Guard or motor car Conductor. Supervision exercised from Seend. Originally to have been called 'Wraggs Wharf'. Further reading – The Devizes Branch, Picton.

BROMLEY HALT

Situated between Brettell Lane and Himley. Opened 11th May 1925, with up and down platforms each 250 ft. long with shelters and steps to the road. Closed 31st October 1932.

BROOK STREET HALT

Situated on the Rhos-Wynn branch. Single platform opened 1st May 1905. Closed 22nd March 1915.

BROUGHTON GIFFORD HALT

Between Melksham and Holt Junction. Up and down platforms opened 29th October 1905.

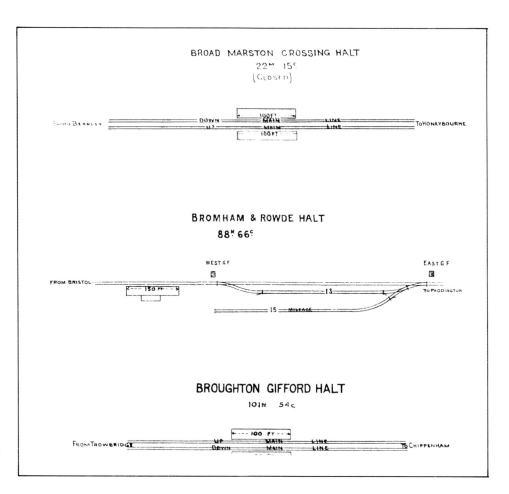

Bromham and Rowde in latter days; the new shelter presumably put up for the timber or agricultural traffic. Intended to have been called 'Wraggs Wharf,' a private siding provided for timber handling and milk was also dealt with.

Collection Brian Hilton

BRYMBO WEST CROSSING HALT

Situated between Brymbo and Coed Poeth. Opened 20th March 1905. Timber up and down platforms with a wooden booking hall and waiting rooms on the up side. No buildings on the other platform. In the 1920s a 'Halt Attendant' was provided to cover the middle turn of duty whilst outside these hours the signalman from the nearby box attended to trains. Closed 1st January 1931.

BRYNCELYNOG HALT

Situated between Arenig and Trawsfyndd. Single platform opened 13th March 1939.

BRYNGWYN HALT

Believed opened on 1st July 1863 with a wooden platform of standard height. A lean-to shelter was also provided. Between Llanfechain and Llanfyllin on the Cambrian railway, this was one of the original two 'flag' stations on the former Cambrian line, where the indication for the driver to stop was given by a signal exhibited on the platform. It is not clear when the device was removed. From 1923 the GWR designated it a Halt although this was only indicated on the rear of the notice board. Further reading – Cambrian Album. Ian Allan.

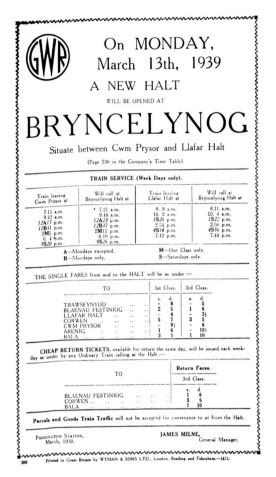

GWR

On MONDAY, March 13th, 1939

A NEW HALT

WILL BE OPENED AT

BRYNCELYNOG

Situate between Cwm Prysor and Llafar Halt

(Page 238 in the Company's Time Table.)

TRAIN SERVICE (Week Days only).

Train leaving Cwm Prysor at	Will call at Bryncelynog Halt at	Train leaving Llafar Halt at	Will call at Bryncelynog Halt at
7.15 a.m.	A 7.21 a.m.	8. 9 a.m.	8.11 a.m.
9.42 a.m.	9.48 a.m.	10. 2 a.m.	10. 4 a.m.
12A17 p.m.	12A23 p.m.	1S20 p.m.	1S22 p.m.
12B31 p.m.	12B37 p.m.	2.54 p.m.	2.56 p.m.
2M5 p.m.	2M11 p.m.	4S54 p.m.	4S56 p.m.
6. 4 p.m.	6.10 p.m.	7.42 p.m.	7.44 p.m.
9S20 p.m.	9S26 p.m.		

A—Mondays excepted.   M—One Class only.
B—Mondays only.   S—Saturdays only.

THE SINGLE FARES from and to the HALT will be as under :—

TO	1st Class.		3rd Class.	
	s.	d.	s.	d.
TRAWSFYNYDD	—	8	—	5
BLAENAU FESTINIOG	2	5	1	6
LLAFAR HALT	—	4	—	2½
CORWEN	5	7	3	5
CWM PRYSOR	—	9½	—	6
ARENIG	1	6	—	10½
BALA	3	1	1	10

CHEAP RETURN TICKETS, available for return the same day, will be issued each week-day as under by any Ordinary Train calling at the Halt :—

TO	Return Fares.	
	3rd Class.	
	s.	d.
BLAENAU FESTINIOG	1	6
CORWEN	3	5
BALA	1	10

Parcels and Goods Train Traffic will not be accepted for conveyance to or from the Halt.

PADDINGTON STATION,   JAMES MILNE,
March, 1939.   General Manager.

300   Printed in Great Britain by WYMAN & SONS LTD., London, Reading and Fakenham.—147L.

Burwarton, on the former C.M & D.P. Railway, depicted in 1938 just one year before closure to passengers. All of the stopping places on this line were designated 'halts' by the GWR although it is not believed that any bore the designation on the nameboard.

Roger Carpenter Collection

Burn Halt served the two locations referred to on the nameboard as well as a collection of nearby farms. The white edging to the shelter was originally provided as a guide to passengers during the strict wartime blackout. Again concrete is apparent although this time timber was retained for the shelter.

Lens of Sutton

Burrator and Sheepstor Halt on the Princetown branch, one of the most beautiful, if remote, on the whole system. The platform and hut were of timber and the location popular, with walkers and hikers intent on the southern slopes of Dartmoor. From the platform it was possible to gain a grandstand view of the nearby Burrator reservoir, which had been the original reason for the construction of the stopping place in 1924.

Lens of Sutton

BURRATOR & SHEEPSTOR HALT. G.W.R.

The branch train from Yelverton to Princetown approaching the Halt. A network of paths and walkways criss-crossed the area and one of these can be seen at the end of the platform.

Lens of Sutton

BRYNNA PLATFORM

Unadvertised stopping place between Pencoed and Llantrisant. Staggered platforms completed 28th November 1918, though believed to have been in use from October 1918. Renamed Bryn-y-Gwynon Platform from 3rd March 1919. It may also have been referred to as Brynna Colliery Platform.

BRYN-Y-GWYNON PLATFORM

See previous entry.

BULLO CROSS HALT

Situated between Newham and Cinderford Single platform opened 3rd August 1907.

BULWARK HALT

22nd March 1928 – proposal for halt between Chepstow and Portskewett at an estimated cost of £308 – not proceeded with.

BURGHFIELD ROAD HALT

13th March 1928 – proposal for halt between Southcote Junction (Reading) and Mortimer- not proceeded with.

BURLISH HALT

Situated between Bewdley and Southport. Authorised on 31st October 1929 with electric lighting at an estimated cost of £430 (£300 engineering, £80 C.M.E. £50 land). Single platform on west side of the line, opened 31st March 1930.

BURN HALT

Between Cadeleigh and Thorverton. Opened 26th January 1929 with nameboard proclaiming 'Burn Halt for Butterleigh'. Provided with a single platform of stone and concrete blocks surmounted by a wooden lean-to shelter. Control of the halt was exercised from Cadeleigh. Further reading – The Exe Valley Railway, Kingfisher.

BURRATOR HALT

See next entry.

BURRATOR PLATFORM

On single line between Dousland and Princetown. Opened for public services from 18th May 1925 though it had existed as an unadvertised workmen's platform from 4th February 1924. Wooden platforms supported on heavy timber trestles. At one end was a wooden hut used as a waiting room with the approach to the platform via 'kissing gates'. Renamed Burrator Halt in 1929 and at an unknown date 'Burrator and Sheeps Tor.' Control exercised from Yelverton. Further reading – The Tavistock, Launceston & Princetown Railways, Oakwood.

BURRATOR AND SHEEPS TOR (HALT)

See entry for Burrator Platform, above.

BURWARTON HALT

Sited between Stottesdon and Ditton Priors on the Cleobury Mortimer and Ditton Priors Railway. Opened 21st November 1908 and designated a 'Halt' from 1st October 1923, although the suffix is not believed to have been carried on the nameboards. Low gravel platforms were provided with the usual small wooden building. The level of the platform was later raised, by the GWR, although still not to the standard height. Closed to passenger traffic on 26th September 1938 and to goods and parcels on 11th September 1939. Further reading – The Cleobury Mortimer & Ditton Priors Railway, OPC.

Bullo Cross Halt between Newnham and Cinderford, which opened in 1907. The photograph was taken over forty years later in 1949 and yet the platform retains its timber construction.
Lens of Sutton

Bullo Cross from the opposite direction in 1946 – the cross bracing of the platform is apparent, as is the crude yet effective method of supporting the rear of the pagoda, on sleepers and blocks.

N. Webb Collection

Two views of the single platform Burlish Halt near Stourport, the Burlish branch running behind the shelter. This is the halt very much in its last years, the pagoda clearly rickety.

N. Webb Collection

Cattistock in 1964.

Collection Brian Hilton

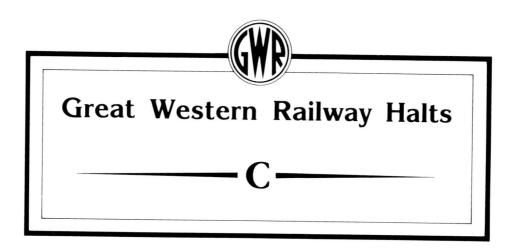

CADOXTON TERRACE HALT

Situated between Neath Riverside and Cildrew. Single platform opened 18th March 1929.

CAEDYAH HALT

Between Overton-on-Dee and Bangor-on-Dee. Single platform opened 30th June 1932. Temporarily closed between 10th June 1940 and 6th May 1946 presumably as a war-time economy. Renamed Cloy Halt very shortly after opening.

CALDICOT HALT

Up and down timber platforms with shelters at the east end, provided between Chepstow and Severn Tunnel Junction, 150 ft. by 8 ft. Access was effected from a nearby level crossing. Opened 12th September 1932 although not shown in engineering department records as authorised until 6th October 1932, at 'an estimated cost of £280.' 'Benacre Halt' is believed to be the name originally intended for here. Despite the close proximity of the former Bristol & South Wales Union main line at this point, no additional platforms were provided on these latter tracks.

CAME BRIDGE HALT

Between Dorchester and Upwey. Up and down platforms opened 1st July 1905 serving nearby golf links as well as two villages. Sometimes referred to as Cam Bridge Halt. Renamed Monkton and Came Halt on 1st October 1905.

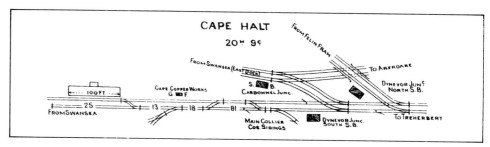

CAPE HALT

Unadvertised stopping place between Jersey Marine and Court Sart, used by workmen at Cape Copper Works. Opening date not reported. Renamed 'Cape Platform' in 1920 and out of use by 11th September 1933.

CAPEL BANGOR

On the narrow gauge Vale of Rheidol railway, between Aberystwyth and Devil's Bridge. Ground level platforms, shelters and sidings, opened 22nd December 1902. Closed at various times from the winter of 1931. Fully re-opened from summer 1945. Halt suffix not carried. Further reading – The Vale of Rheidol Light Railway, Wild Swan.

CAPEL CELWYN HALT

Single platform between Frongogh and Arenig, opened 1st December 1930.

CAPE PLATFORM

See entry for Cape Halt.

CARADOG FALLS HALT

Situated between Trawscoed and Strata Florida. Single platform opened 5th September 1932.

'CARBIS HALT'

This name does not appear in official registers despite appearing in an official photograph! It is possibly the similarly sounding Carbis Bay station on the St. Ives branch, temporarily renamed by the Publicity Department.   (see photo p.50)

CARDIFF MAINDY ROAD NORTH HALT

See Maindy Road North Halt.

CARDIFF NINIAN PARK PLATFORM

See Ninian Park Platform.

CARDONNEL HALT

Situated between Neath Abbey and Briton Ferry Road. Up and down platforms opened 1st June 1905. Closed 28th September 1936.

CARREGHOFA HALT

Single platform opened 11th April 1938, between Llanymynech and Llansantffraidd.

CASHES GREEN HALT

Located between Stroud and Stonehouse. Up and down platforms, opened 22nd January 1930, though does not appear in Engineering Department minutes until 19th October 1930, which reported that material from the closed Chalvey Halt on the Windsor branch was used in its construction. Both platforms timber with basic shelters, fencing, nameboards, gates and lighting. Estimated cost of construction £185.

CASSINGTON HALT

Opened 9th March 1936 on the north side of the single line with 100 ft. platform and timber shelter. The halt, between Yarnton and Evesham, was later moved to a new site, a little to the west and on the south side of the line. At this time a concrete platform was in use although it is not certain if this was an original item. The resiting of the halt was necessitated by the rebuilding of an adjacent road bridge allowing passengers easy access to the platform below. Certain reports refer to the resiting having occurred in 1947/48 although there is evidence to suggest it may have taken place in the late 1930s. Unstaffed, and included with Evesham for accounting purposes. Further reading – The Fairford Branch, Oakwood.

Cardonell Halt. G.W.R.

Caldicot Halt looking towards Gloucester. The photograph makes an interesting comparison with plans, which bear no reference to a shelter on the up platform. It is not certain if this feature was original or a later change.
Lens of Sutton

This is (supposedly) Cardonnell Halt on the Vale of Neath line, though with only one platform apparent.
Great Western Trust

Carreghofa Halt, with basic arrangements. A good impression is gained of yet another shelter variant; this one has a something of a valance above the opening.
Lens of Sutton

CASTLE BAR PARK HALT

Between West Ealing and Greenford. Up and down platforms, opened on 1st May 1904. Additional facilities authorised on 25th November 1937, comprising foot-bridge between the platforms, gates, alterations to the office, fencing and telegraph route. Total cost of changes £820. For accountancy purposes it was included with either Southall or Greenford.

CASTLEBYTHE HALT

Located on the line between Letterston and Puncheston a single platform was opened to traffic on 24th September 1928. The halt closed on 25th October 1937. Further reading — The Railways of Pembrokeshire, H.G.Walters.

CASTLE CAEREINION

Welshpool and Llanfair narrow gauge railway. Opened 4th April 1903. Closed to passengers from 9th February 1931.

CATHAYS BRIDGE HALT

Single short platform 65 ft. long on the double line between Cardiff and Llandaff on the Taff Vale Railway, near to Crockhers-town Upper Signal Box and served by up trains only. Access was accomplished via a gate and some steps leading down to the road below. A letter sent by the Taff Vale Company to the Board of Trade on 15th June 1906 sought permission to proceed with the construction of the halt and opening was believed to have taken place the following month. Inspected by the Board of Trade on 10th November 1906, which commented that a name board either within a lamp or nearby should be provided. Renamed Cathays (Woodville Road) Platform sometime after 1906 and then Cathays (Woodville Road) Halt from 10th July 1922.

CATHAYS (WOODVILLE ROAD) HALT

See entry for Cathays Bridge Halt.

CATHAYS (WOODVILLE ROAD) PLATFORM

See entry for Cathays Bridge Halt.

CATTISTOCK HALT

Authorised on 21st May 1931, wooden up and down platforms, waiting shelters and

Cassington Halt in its second location, with No. 2221 running at the head of a Fairford to Oxford train. The waiting shelter is seen to advantage; again it has an ornate valance. The lamps are of the oil type and a set of wooden steps was kept at the halt, to enable the porter/guard to attend to cleaning and lighting. It is not known if the concrete was an original feature, dating back to 1936. Access was via the path leading from the road bridge.
Lens of Sutton

Looking north through Castle Bar Park Halt towards Greenford provides an interesting view of the gradients on this line. The provision of the halt shelters at one end of the platform was by no means uncommon.
Roger Carpenter Collection

paraffin vapour lighting, between Evershot and Maiden Newton. Estimated cost £636. Opened 3rd August 1931.

CAUSELAND

Sited between Liskeard and Looe. Opened 11th September 1879. Single platform, unstaffed with supervision exercised from Looe. Halt suffix believed not displayed.

CEFN COED COLLIERY HALT

Situated between Llanishen and Caerphilly on the Rhymney Railway. Timber up and down platforms 100 ft. x 9 ft. x 3 ft. provided on slightly different levels with access via pathways leading to a road overbridge. The stopping place is first referred to as under construction on 23rd December 1914 and was inspected by the Board of Trade on 6th August 1915. This would tend to imply it was opened by that date although official records refer to an opening in October 1915 – no actual date is given. It is believed that the name was originally intended to have been 'Tunnel South Halt'. It was altered to 'Cefn On' at an unknown date.

CELTIC HALT

Single platform on the Port Talbot to Pontyrhyll line. Unadvertised and serving nearby colliery. Opening date not reported but out of use by September 1938.

An enigma, a halt which does not seem to exist! The answer would appear to be a 1930s publicity photograph, taken by the GWR, though the location remains a mystery.

National Railway Museum

The basic stopping place at Causeland on the Liskeard and Looe line; it was designated a 'Halt' by the GWR even though the suffix was not displayed. The use of what appears to be stone for the platform edging is unusual whilst the permanent way staff are working on the light section flat bottom rail typical of this branch.

LGRP

CELTIC LOWER PLATFORM

See Cwm Cedfyn Rhondda Halt.

CELYNEN HALT

Situated between Abercarn and Newbridge. Authorised on 8th October 1931 to serve South Celynen Colliery. Consisting of up and down platform, approach road and steps, waiting shelters on up side, fencing, gates and electric lighting. Estimated total cost of £565. Opened 14th August 1933. Renamed "Celynen South Halt' in April 1936. May have also carried the name 'Celynen Colliers Halt' for a period between 1933 and 1936.

CELYNEN NORTH HALT

On the Western Valleys line between Crumlin Low Level and Newbridge, an island platform authorised on 29th November 1935 serving up and down lines. Name and notice boards, gate and lighting. The footbridge from Usk was taken down and re-erected at the new stopping place at an estimated cost of £1080. Referred to as a 'workmen's halt' and not advertised in timetables. Brought into use on 10th August 1936.

CELYNEN SOUTH HALT

See entry for Celynen Halt.

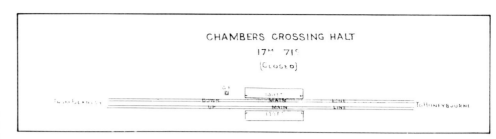

CHAMBERS CROSSING HALT
17ᴹ 71ᶜ
(CLOSED)

CEMETERY HALT

Unadvertised single platform on former joint LNW/Rhymney line. Situated between Rhymney and Rhymney Bridge. Believed to have been used solely by colliers. Opening date not reported but known to have been post-1895. Out of use by September 1928.

CEMMAES

Situated between Cemmes Road and Dinas Mawddwy on the Mawddwy Railway. Single platform opened in 1865 by the Cambrian Railway with the name of Cemmes but closed on 17th April 1901. Re-opened with name Cemmaes from 31st July 1911 and finally closed again from 1st January 1931.

CHALVEY HALT

Between Slough and Windsor. Authorised on 24th February 1929 at an estimated cost of £840. Up and down platforms, shelters and steps to public road. Opened 6th May 1929. Closed on 7th July 1930, but materials re-erected at the new Cashes Green Halt in the Stroud valley.

CHAMBERS CROSSING HALT

Up and down platforms, between Milcote and Stratford-on-Avon, opened 17th October 1904, closed 14th July 1916.

CHARLTON HALT

Between Filton Junction and Henbury. Authorised on 2nd July 1909 at an estimated cost of £304. Opened 9th May 1910 with a single timber platform and pagoda shelter. Closed 22nd March 1915.

CHEDWORTH

Situated between Foss Cross and Withington on the Midland & South Western Junction Railway. Opened 1st October 1892 and reduced to Halt status from 8th July 1928 with singling of the line. Staff however retained. Halt suffix not displayed. Further reading – The Midland & South Western Junction Rly, Wild Swan.

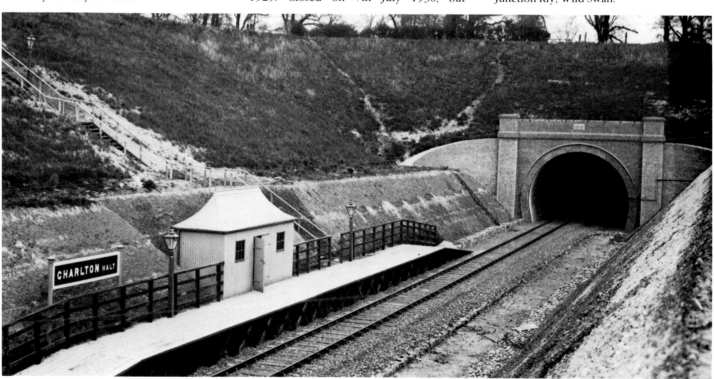

Charlton Halt pictured almost new, looking towards Filton. Access was via a footpath and steps, visible to the left, leading up from behind the pagoda.

National Railway Museum

CHELTENHAM HIGH STREET HALT

Between Cheltenham Malvern Road and Bishops Cleeve. Up and down platforms opened 1st October 1908. Closed 30th April 1917.

CHETNOLE HALT

Located between Yetminster and Evershot. Authorised on 29th June 1933 with staggered up and down platforms 150 ft. by 7 ft. 6 inches; constructed of timber, shelters, steps to dissecting road bridge, lamp hut, gates, drainage and lighting. Estimated cost £410. Opened 11th September 1933.

CHILTON HALT

On the Cleobury Mortimer and Ditton Priors Railway. Opened, between Cleobury Town and Denton Ford, around June 1917 possibly, at first, as a private platform. Closed 11th September 1939. Parcels traffic handled. No name board provided. Further reading – The Cleobury Mortimer & Ditton Priors Light Rly, OPC.

CHISELDON CAMP HALT

Opened 1st December 1930, between Ogbourne and Chiseldon. Single 100 ft. timber platform and shelter. Unstaffed and supervised from Chiseldon Station. Electric lighting provided with a switch in the shelter. Further reading – The Midland & South Western Junction Rly, Wild Swan.

CHITTENING HALT

See Chittening Factory Platform.

CHITTENING PLATFORM

See Chittening Factory Platform.

CHITTENING FACTORY PLATFORM

Situated between Henbury and Avonmouth, for workmens use and unadvertised. Opened 13th November 1918 and closed 11th October 1923. Up and down platforms, constructed from material reputedly removed from the nearby Hallen Halt. Re-opened as 'Chittening Platform,' again for workmens trains, on 27th October 1941 and for other passengers use on 31st May 1948. Also referred to as 'Chittening Halt.' Between 1915 and 13th November 1918 a location 'Chittening Siding' is also referred to at the same location, alleged to have been used by workmens trains. Further reading – Lines to Avonmouth, OPC.

CHITTENING SIDING

See Chittening Factory Platform.

CHRISTIAN MALFORD HALT

Between Dauntsey and Chippenham. Authorised on 29th April 1926 and opened on 18th October 1926 with 150 ft. up and down platforms, shelters on each platform, pathways and steps leading from the Christian Malford to Foxham road. Estimated cost of £650 including necessary earthworks. Opened 18th October 1926. Electric lighting authorised on 7th October 1937 at an estimated cost of £127. Porter provided between 9.30 a.m. and 6 p.m. Monday to Saturday, after which time the guard of any train calling at the halt was

Chedworth looking north towards Andoversford on the former MSWJ system, before its reduction to 'Halt'. After 1928 only the former down platform remained in use for all trains.

Lens of Sutton

From the dissecting road bridge, a view of one of the platforms at Chetnole Halt. Surmounting the platform is yet another type of wooden shelter whilst beyond is what appears to be a lamp hut and a permanent way cabin.

Lens of Sutton

Another stopping place on the former MSWJ route, although this time instigated by the GWR was Chiseldon Camp Halt and as the name implies it served a nearby army camp. Electricity was accordingly available from the outset and there was no need to resort to the older style of oil lamps.

D. Thompson

responsible for collecting tickets, etc. Supervision exercised from both Dauntsey and Chippenham.

CHUDLEIGH KNIGHTON HALT

Authorised on 31st January 1924 at an estimated cost of £300. Single masonry platform with pagoda shelter, between Heathfield and Chudleigh. Opened 9th June 1924 and unstaffed. Further reading – The Teign Valley Line, Oakwood.

CHURCH VILLAGE HALT

Situated between Llantwit and Tonteg Halt on the Taff Vale Railway. Single platform and unstaffed. Halt suffix dropped from 14th March 1932.

CHURN HALT

Opened in June 1888. Situated between Upton & Blewbury and Compton. Unstaffed from the time of opening but with a siding for the military authorities in connection with nearby army ranges. Designated a halt by the GWR from 1923. Temporary closure from 4th August 1942 to 8th March 1943 when the single platform was converted to an island in connection with the doubling of the former D.N. & S. line and the siding removed. No road access. For accounting purposes included with neighbouring Compton Station. Further reading – The Didcot, Newbury & Southampton Rly, Wild Swan.

CILIAU AERON HALT

Single platform between Felin Fach and Crossways. Opened to passengers 12th May

Christian Malford Halt on the main line between Dauntsey and Chippenham. Again there is variation in the type of shelter, one no doubt welcomed by passengers, in this exposed position on the Wiltshire plains.

D. Thompson

Chudlegh Knighton Halt, from the occupation crossing. Note the use of concrete, including the supports to the nameboard. The pagoda however retains its corrugated material – see Newbury West Fields Halt.

Lens of Sutton

Downgraded from a station, this is Church Village Halt on the former Taff Vale railway, between Llantwit and Tonteg Halt.

Lens of Sutton

1911 and designated a halt some time after 1927.

CILFREW PLATFORM

Situated between Crynant and Neath on the Neath and Brecon Railway. Opening details uncertain. Closed 1st May 1895 and replaced by a new station nearby, named Cilfrew.

CLEARBROOK HALT

Situated between Bickleigh and Yelverton. Opened 29th October 1928 with small waiting shed. No permanent staff although in the morning a 'lad porter' would walk from the supervising station at Yelverton with a ticket box and return on a mid-morning train. Apart from passengers, there was some traffic in cakes for a local shop, which the porter would load onto a barrow for delivery. Further reading – The Tavistock, Launceston and Princetown Rlys, Oakwood.

CLEOBURY NORTH CROSSING

Between Burwarton and Ditton Priors on the C.M. & D. P. Railway. Opened 19th November 1900. Parcels traffic handled. Single low platform with small concrete shelter typical of this railway. Designated a Halt from 1st October 1923. Closed to passengers from 26th September 1938. Further reading – The Cleobury Mortimer & Ditton Priors Light Rly, OPC.

CLEOBURY TOWN

Cleobury Mortimer & Ditton Priors Light Railway, between Cleobury Mortimer and Stottesdon. Low platforms, opened 19th November 1900. Parcels traffic handled. Designated a Halt from 1st October 1923 although the suffix was not displayed. Closed to passengers from 26th September 1938. Further reading – The Cleobury Mortimer & Ditton Priors Light Rly, OPC.

CLOY HALT

See entry for Caedyah Halt.

CLYDACH COURT HALT

See entry for Clydach Court Platform.

A superb view of Clyne Halt taken on 8th September 1926. The camera has captured several interesting features of the construction, including old sleepers for the platform edging.

National Railway Museum

CLYDACH COURT PLATFORM

Single platform between Pontypridd and Ynysybwl on the Taff Vale Railway. Opened in July 1917 and renamed Clydach Court Halt on 2nd October 1922.

CLYDACH VALE PLATFORM

Single platform beyond Penygraig on the Ely Valley line. Unadvertised, and used by miners some time after 1897. Abandoned by September 1926.

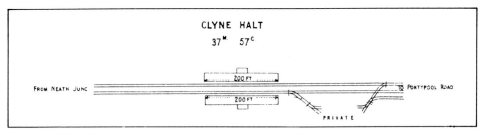

CLYNE HALT

Situated between Resolven and Aberdylais. Opened 1st June 1905. Up and down platforms with standard pagoda shelters.

CODFORD CAMP

Military platform on camp line from Codford station. Believed in use between 1914 and 1923.

This series of views of Clyne was supposed to have been taken as a result of an accident to a passenger. Further details unfortunately are not given. As well as a fine portrait of the halt itself this photograph provides for a wonderful illustration of a typical occupation crossing and the standard notice, warning of a forty shilling penalty for failure to close the gate after opening.

National Railway Museum

A final view of Clyne Halt showing the buildings to advantage. The shelter appears to display the same hue all over and was probably therefore in standard 'dark stone' livery.

National Railway Museum

COED ELY HALT

Opened 13th July 1925 with up and down platforms, between Llantrisant and Penygraig. Halt suffix not shown on nameboards.

COLD HARBOUR HALT

Opened 23rd February 1929, on single line between Tiverton Junction and Uffculme.

COLEFORD JUNCTION PLATFORM

Unadvertised platform on single line between Parkend and Speech House Road. In use by workmen c.1899. Out of use at an unreported date. Further reading – The Severn & Wye Railway, Wild Swan.

COLLINGBOURNE KINGSTON HALT

Situated between Collingbourne and Grafton on the former MSWJ system. Authorised on 21st January 1932 with timber up and down platforms, small corrugated waiting shelters, steps, paths to road,

Codford Camp on Salisbury Plain, termination of a military line built from the W.S. & W. station of the same name. The very nature of military lines makes it difficult to be precise over the sites of actual stopping places and it is likely more than one may have been involved.

The diminutive Cold Harbour Halt on the single line between Tiverton Junction and Uffculme, where the platform could accommodate just a single coach.

Lens of Sutton

Tickets could be obtained at Cold Harbour Halt from the signalman, for which purpose a small ticket window and canopy shelter were provided at the rear of the box.

Lens of Sutton

Collingbourne Kingston Halt, looking north towards Grafton, in its last days and yet little altered from when built. Passenger access was via pathways leading to the road bridge.

D. Thompson

oil hut, name boards, fencing, gates and lighting. Public access between the two platforms via a nearby road overbridge. Opened 1st April 1932. Unstaffed with tickets available from a local agent. Electric lighting later provided, estimated cost £355. Further reading – The Midland & South Western Junction Rly, Wild Swan.

COLTHROP CROSSING HALT

2nd March 1928 proposal for a halt between Thatcham and Midgham intended to serve nearby papermills. Not proceeded with.

Two views of Commins Coch Halt (top and middle) where the 'Halt' suffix was only displayed on the rear. Again there would appear to be a non standard type of shelter, with a small nameboard displayed above the entrance.
Lens of Sutton (both)

The remains of Combe Hay halt, which closed completely from 25th September 1925.
Mowat Collection

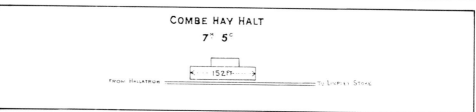

COMBE HAY HALT
7ᴹ 5ᶜ

152 FT

FROM HALLATROW — — — TO LIMPLEY STOKE

COMBE HALT

Situated between Handborough and Finstock Halt. Authorised on 14th February 1935 with staggered up and down platforms of timber, 150 ft. by 7 ft. 6 ins, paths to road, shelters, lamp hut, name and notice boards, fencing, gates and lighting. Estimated total cost £516. Opened 8th July 1935. Both platform surfaces made up of old sleepers without any further covering.

COMBE HAY HALT

Situated between Dunkerton and Limpley Stoke, built by outside contractors and opened 9th May 1910. Single platform and shelter. Temporary closure between 23rd March 1915 and 9th July 1923. Closed completely from 25th September 1925. Further reading – The Camerton Branch, Wild Swan.

COMMERCIAL STREET PLATFORM

Single platform serving down line only between Aberdare Low Level and High Level stations. Opening date not reported but closed from June 1912.

COMMINS COCH HALT

Single platform situated between Llanbrynmain and Cemmes Road. Opened 19th October 1931.

Another official view, this time of Combe Halt, on 6th November 1935. The GWR seemed to have difficulty in correctly spelling the name of several of its stopping places. This was one, where 'Coombe' was often substituted. Notice the staggered platforms apparently made necessary by the nearby embankment.

National Railway Museum

A poor quality but rare view of Coombe Junction with the main line carried across the valley on the viaduct in the distance. Of particular interest is the position of the nameboard, above the entrance to the shelter, and clearly not of original GWR design.

Lens of Sutton

COMPTON HALT

Situated between Wombourn and Tettenhall. Originally authorised in 1908 under the name of 'Compton, Wightwick & Tettenhall Wood Halt'. Opened 11th May 1925 with 250 ft. platform, shelter, lamp hut and access footpath to public road. Closed 31st October 1932. Further reading – The Railway to Wombourn, Uralia Press.

COOLE PILOT HALT

Situated between Audlem and Nantwich. Authorised on 27th June 1935 at an estimated cost of £275. Up and down platforms, opened 17th August 1935.

COOMBE JUNCTION

Between Liskeard and Looe; other details unclear although known to have been unstaffed in 1939 and under the supervision of Liskeard.

COOMBES HOLLOWAY HALT

Situated between Old Hill and Halesowen. Opened 1st July 1905. First referred to in a letter from the GWR to the Board of Trade of 5th June 1905 requesting permission to construct and bring into use the stopping place, consisting of a single platform 150 ft. by 6 ft. by 3 ft. 'with access via a 1 in 5 inclined ramp leading to Gorsby Road.' It was subsequently inspected by Colonel Yorke, on 2nd August 1905 and deemed

'.....suitable for motor car traffic.' In April 1913 the position of the platform was altered from the down or east side to the up side of the single line, with no record of a further Board of Trade inspection. Sometimes referred to as 'Coombs Holloway Halt' the stopping place closed on 5th December 1927.

COPPERHOUSE HALT

Situated on what was then the single line between Gwinear Road and Hayle. Opened 1st July 1905, closed 1st May 1908.

COPPER PIT HALT

See Copper Pit Platform.

COPPER PIT PLATFORM

Located between Plas Marl and Morrison. Reported open on February 1915 – but see comments below. Single timber platform provided of standard height, 150 ft. by 10 ft,

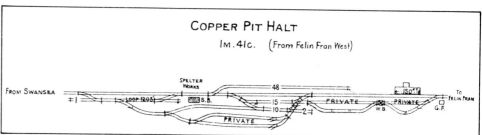

Copper Pit Platform in its final years, with the nameboard modified to read 'Copper Pit Halt'. The pagoda was of standard design and was probably unlit within, where there would be a simple wooden bench around three sides.

Mowat Collection

with waiting shed and footpath to the road overbridge. The Board of Trade was informed of the new stopping place by the GWR on 20th December 1914 although it was not stated to be ready for inspection until 6th December 1915. At this time Board of Trade reports refer to the location as 'Copper Pit Halt' although GWR records refer to '.....Platform' with a renaming to 'Copper Pit Halt' some time after 1939.

CORRWYG MERTHYR NAVIGATION COLLIERY HALT

Unadvertised colliers' halt at the end of the branch from Tonmawr Halt, Port Talbot Railway. In use by 1920 and closed by 1930. Due to changes in colliery ownership also referred to at unreported dates as 'Torybanwen Colliery Halt' and Whitworth Halt.'

CORYATES HALT

Situated between Upwey and Portesham. Original facilities a 100 ft. by 14 ft. platform, 14 inches high. Opened 1st May 1906 and located on the south side of the line with an access pathway running east to a road underbridge. The GWR first informed the Board of Trade of the new stopping place on 3rd April 1906; on 15th May it was ready for inspection and on 24th August Colonel Yorke attended and commented as follows:
'I have inspected the new motor Halte at Coryates on the Abbotsbury single line branch of the GWR. The halt consists of a single platform 100' x 7' and 14" above rail level on which lamp and name boards have been provided but no shelter. The cars which are to use this halt have end doors which are provided with special folding steps, reaching when open, to the level of the platform. The arrangement being satisfactory I can recommend its sanction for public use....'
It will be noted that on some inspections the Board of Trade used the spelling 'Halt' and at other times 'Halte'. Colonel Yorke continued:
'The company do not seem to have fixed upon a standard height for the platforms of halts. In many cases the platforms are 3' high and in others 14" high. The former are suitable for ordinary carriages with side doors but the latter are suitable only for special motor coaches with side doors and folding steps and should be used by such coaches...'
Coryates was unstaffed, with supervision exercised from Upwey. Perhaps as a direct consequence of the Colonel's comments the platform was raised to standard height in 1907. A pagoda shelter was also provided at some time after the initial opening. It is reported that a considerable amount of milk traffic was handled. Further reading – The Abbotsbury Branch, Wild Swan.

CORYTON HALT

Situated between Whitchurch and Tongwynlais. Opened 1st March 1911 with a masonry platform. Halt suffix dropped shortly afterwards but restored from 1st July 1924. In connection with singling of line authorised on 7th October 1926, a new platform 200 ft. long with shelter was provided on the former up side.

COSFORD AERODROME HALT

Between Albrighton and Shifnal. Approval for construction given by GWR on 25th November 1937 to serve the RAF aerodrome and cadet school. Opened 31st March 1938 and equipped with up and down platforms 200 ft. long, steps, path to road, shelters, booking office, name and notice boards, fencing gates, drainage and lighting. Cost of construction estimated at

Coryates Halt on the Abbotsbury branch. As depicted the pagoda shelter is of the standard type although in later years part of the front was cut away, so that churns could be placed in the shade. This would appear to have been unusual and no similar modifications have been located.

£660 plus a further £25 for moving telegraph poles and wires. Originally to have been called 'Neachley Halt'. Extra work approved on 6th October 1938 with extension of platforms together with provision of loops, sidings and a private siding connection for the Air Ministry. Estimated cost of new work £14,204. Additional expenditure of £175 on 23rd March 1939 when an extra platform support was provided. Authorisation for a major rebuilding of facilities given on 29th June 1939 at a cost of £4,130, to include a Station Master's house. After this the place was re-designated a station, 'Cosford', from 28th October 1940.

COUND HALT

Originally to have been called 'Cound Lodge Halt,' a single platform opened 4th August 1934, between Cressage and Berrington. Authorised on 31st May 1934 at an estimated cost of £172.

COVE HALT

Situated between Bampton and Tiverton. Although shown as officially open from 9th June 1924, it is suggested the site may have been in use as 'Cove Siding Halt' from March 1923. At this time it is reported as having a single low platform. This was replaced by one of conventional height, with pagoda shelter, some time after 1926. Unstaffed. Further reading – The Exe Valley Railway, Kingfisher.

COVE SIDING HALT

See Cove Halt.

Coryton halt in its final years, with the pagoda shelter just visible amongst the bushes in the distance. This section of line, formerly double track, was singled in 1926.
Lens of Sutton

Cove Halt on the Exe Valley branch which served the local village as well as a nearby quarry. From the photograph the shelter would appear to have a more pronounced pitch than was usual.
Lens of Sutton

The single platform at Cound Halt on the now abandoned northern portion of the Severn Valley line. The stopping place was situated on the down side of the line and was once, evidently, to have been called 'Cound Lodge Halt'.
Lens of Sutton

COXBANK HALT

Located between Adderley and Audlem. Authorised on 31st May 1934 with up and down platforms 80 ft. long, steps to road, overbridge, footpath and steps to the Market Drayton Road. Also shelters, name and notice boards, fencing, gates and lighting. Estimated total cost of £368. Opened 23rd June 1934. Referred to in certain records as 'Coxbench Halt.'

CRAIGLONG BRIDGE HALT

Situated between Burry Port and Trimsaren Road. Opened 1st February 1932 with a single platform approached by steps leading down from road level.

CREECH ST. MICHAEL HALT

On the four track main line between Durston and Taunton. Authorised on 28th June 1928 with up and down platforms 300 ft. by 8 ft. with alcoves, ticket offices, footpaths to public roads, steps to bridge and lighting. Estimated cost of £582. Opened 13th August 1928. The floral display of the gardens at this stopping place were the subject of much praise from passengers and were featured in the 'Great Western Magazine.'

CROSS HANDS HALT

Opened 9th July 1928, between Pilning Junction and Severn Beach. Single 150 ft. platform. Unstaffed but with tickets issued by a local agent. Supervising station, Pilning, and paraffin vapour lighting provided. The guard of the last train booked to call was responsible for collecting the lamps from the halt and handing these to the signalman upon arrival at Pilning.

One of the few halts on a four track main line was at Creech St. Michael, in many ways more akin to a full station. Again advantage has been taken of the nearby road bridge, affording access between the two platforms.

Lens of Sutton

An early view of Cross Hands Halt with yet another variety of shelter. From the curved roof profile of the corrugated building it may well be that such structures were deliberately kept within loading gauge restrictions in order to afford ease of transport to the required site.

Great Western Trust

A later view of the stopping place looking toward Pilning Junction. It can be seen by comparison with the previous photograph that a larger shelter is now in place, on a different site.

Lens of Sutton

CROSSWAYS HALT

Situated between Cilliau Aeron and Aberayron. Single platform opened 8th April 1929.

CRUMLIN VALLEY COLLIERY PLATFORM

Unadvertised stopping place between Hafodyrynys and Pontypool Clarence Street. Up and down platforms in use some time after 1910.

CRYNANT NEW COLLIERY HALT

Unadvertised stopping place on single line between Crynant and Seven Sisters. Came into use some time between 1923 and 1938.

CUTNALL GREEN HALT

Situated between Droitwich Spa and Hartlebury. Authorised on 24th April 1928 and opened in June 1928. Up and down platforms 100 ft. by 8 ft, alcoves, footpaths to public road, mileage siding on up side, coal wharf, weighbridge, fencing and gates. Estimated total cost of £2280. Believed name originally intended to be 'Hampton Lovatt Halt'.

CWMAMAN COLLIERY HALT

Single platform on the Cwmaman branch, opened 1st January 1906. Closed 22nd September 1924. Between 1903 and 1st January 1906, and from 22nd September 1924 until 1932, served as a miners platform.

CWMAMAN CROSSING HALT

Single platform on the Cwmaman branch, opened 1st January 1906. Closed to passengers from 22nd September 1924 but remained in use for miners traffic until 1932.

CWMAVON HALT

Unadvertised miners' stopping place on single line of the former South Wales Mineral Junction branch, close to the R&SB route Cwmavon (Glamorgan) station. Opening date uncertain but believed around 1921. Out of use by 1930. See also entry for 'Maesmelyn Miners Halt.'

CWMBACH HALT

Authorised 26th May 1910, although not opened until 12th July 1914. Up and down platforms between Mountain Ash and Aberdare High Level. Platforms 300 ft long, joined by a footbridge and each with a small corrugated shelter. Estimated cost of facilities £1071. A further entry of 19th February 1913 refers to 'steps to footbridge to be constructed by Aberdare U.D.C.' Revised cost of £1282. It is not clear what items specifically were to be constructed by the U.D.C.

CWM CEDFYN RHONDDA HALT

Unadvertised miners' stopping place between Lletty Brongu and Celtic Halt. Exact location unclear but presumably near to junction with Cwm Cedfyn Rhondda Colliery. Opened some time prior to 1924, for in this year the name was changed to 'Celtic Lower Platform'. Closed after 1930.

CWM COLLIERS PLATFORM

Unadvertised platform on east side of double line between Aberbeeg and Cwm.

A general view of the arrangements at Cutnall Green Halt; the signal box controlled the loops either side of the stopping place. The nameboard bears what appears to be non-standard type lettering.

Lens of Sutton

Believed in use by 1890 and renamed 'Marine Colliery Platform' by 1938.

CWMFFRWD HALT

Situated between Abersychan Low Level and Cwmavon. Opened 13th July 1912 with up and down timber platforms 150 ft. long with shelters. Access from the nearby level crossing. Estimated cost of £377 although actual expenditure was £430.

CWMFFRWDOER HALT

Situated between Pontypool Crane Street and Abersychan on the Eastern Valleys line. Authorised 23rd February 1911 with up and down platforms, shelters, steps and footpaths at an estimated cost of £431. Opened 13th July 1912. Closed 5th May 1941.

CWMNOEL HALT

Single platform situated on the Cwmaman branch. Originally opened to miners traffic in 1903 and authorised on 31st May 1905 to be converted from private colliery platform for public use. Opened for this traffic on 1st January 1906. Closed 22nd September 1924.

CWM PRYSOR

Sited between Arenig and Trawsfynydd. Opened in 1902 although previously certain trains had called upon special request – facilities in this period unknown. From 1902 a 100 ft. wooden platform provided on the down side of the line, with a small timber shelter. Reported that in 1926 staff consisted solely of a gatewoman, who was provided with a cottage adjacent to the level crossing and hard by the south end of the platform. Her wages recorded as 6 shillings per week in 1926 plus a 3/6d bonus. Rental for the cottage 2/9d including rates. Trains stopped upon request by exhibiting a red flag. Up to 4th July 1938 had been a conditional stopping place only.

CWMRHYD-Y-GAU HALT

Unadvertised stopping place between Glyn Neath and Pontwalby Halt, intended for colliers only. Up and down platforms authorised on 25th October 1934 at an estimated cost of £236. Opened 14th January 1935. Closed by October 1945.

No. 4671 at Cwmsyfiog Halt with the 6.08 to New Tredegar in August 1958. Again a non-standard type of building has been provided.

M. Hale

CWMSYFIOG COLLIERY HALT

Single platform previously in use as Cwmsyfiog Station, between Aberbargoed and New Tredegar. Miners halt from 6th December 1937.

CWMSYFIOG HALT

Situated between Aberbargoed and New Tredegar. Single platform opened 5th July 1937.

CYFARTHFA

Workmens halt on the GWR/Rhymney branch from Abercanaid. Brought into use by July 1897. Closed some time after 1915.

CYFRONYDD

Narrow gauge Welshpool and Llanfair Light Railway. Opened 4th April 1903. Closed 9th February 1931.

CYNON PLATFORM

Situated between Cymmer and Pontrhydyfen on the Rhondda and Swansea Bay railway. Up and down platforms opened 10th July 1911. Closed from 2nd October 1911 to October 1912 when it re-opened as 'Cynonville Halt'. 25th October 1912 provision of booking office and waiting room authorised at an estimated cost of £130. Unstaffed from 14th November 1932.

CYNONVILLE HALT

See entry for Cynon Platform.

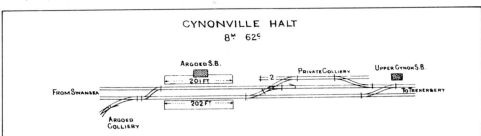

Great Western Railway Halts

D

DANYGRAIG HALT

Up and down platforms opened 11th September 1933, between Swansea East Dock and Briton Ferry Road, to replace the former R. & S.B. Railway station of Danygraig. Closed 28th September 1936.

DARBY END HALT

Up and down platforms, opened 21st August 1905 between Old Hill and Windmill End. Further reading – Railways of the Black Country, Uralia Press.

DAWLISH WARREN

See Warren Halt

DEFIANCE HALT(S)/PLATFORM

See also entry for Defiance Platform. Situated between Saltash and St.Germans. The first reference appears to have been on 22nd February 1905, with the GWR seeking permission from the Board of Trade to 'construct and bring into use this stopping place.' The halt opened on 1st March 1905 and was inspected on 7th June by Colonel Yorke, who commented:

'I have the honour .... I inspected on the 24th March the Defiance Halte near Saltash on the GWR. The line is single, and the halte consists of a single raised platform 150 ft. by 6 ft. wide which has been built by the naval authorities chiefly for the convenience of their officers and men. The platform is reached by two pathways, one for the use of the general public, connecting with the public road and the other leading to the Admiralty landing place. There is a sharp corner on the latter path at which I suggest a short length of post and rail fence be erected to prevent anyone in

Denham Golf Club platform in later years, by which time the original wooden platforms had been replaced by the then standard concrete variant. The corrugated pagoda buildings were retained.

Lens of Sutton

the dark from falling down the steep bank. The company's boundary is the pathway belonging to the naval authority. The company said they would draw the attention of the naval authority to the matter. I recommend that sanction be given to the use of the halte for passenger traffic.' On 31st July 1905 the GWR reported that the required fence had been provided by the Navy.

It is suggested that construction was carried out by sailors from the shore base HMS DEFIANCE to plans provided by the GWR. Before the fence was even completed the GWR again wrote to the Board of Trade, on 14th July 1905, over 'the new Defiance Halt' on the deviation line, between Saltash and St. Germans and its improved facilities. This time a 230ft platform was proposed on each side of the up and down lines, with alcoves at the west end of each platform and steps to the road overbridge.

This was opened on an unknown date, the GWR reporting on 14th May 1906 that the works were ready for inspection. Again Colonel Yorke attended and stated...

'I have inspected the halte for rail motor cars which has been constructed between Saltash and St.Germans on the GWR. The halte consists of two platforms each 350 ft. long, 7 ft. wide and 3 ft. above rail level. Each platform has a small shelter as well as lamps and name boards. The halte is on the new deviation lines between mile 151½ and 152¼. The arrangements being satisfactory I can recommend......'

The original stopping place closed early in 1908.

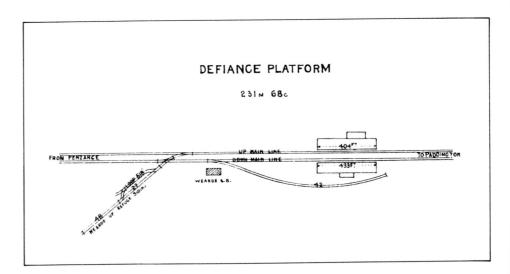

DEFIANCE PLATFORM

The new Defiance Halt (see above) was renamed Defiance Platform from 1st May 1906; additionally, it was reported, parcels traffic was handled. Shortly after opening widening and lengthening of the platforms to 400 ft. was authorised, together with the erection of an alcove on the up side, brought from St. Budeaux and a similar example on the down side, this time from Ford. Estimated cost £263. 9th June 1921 further entry reads: 'provision of shelter at an estimated cost of £250.' 22nd November 1928 lavatory accommodation authorised at estimated cost of £214. Closed 27th October 1930.

DENHAM GOLF CLUB PLATFORM

Situated between Denham and Gerrards Cross on the GW/GC joint line. Opened 22nd July 1912 with timber up and down platforms. It was staffed from the outset with an early and late turn porter, whose wage bill for the years 1936/37/38 was £256, £263 and £271 respectively. Previous to 1936 receipts were included with the Denham account but latterly separate accounting took place allowing an insight into the actual traffic handled. It rose steadily from £1203 in 1936 to £1433 in 1938. The consequent rise in passengers from over 15,000 to just under 21,000 was

H.M.S. Defiance, showing "Defiance Halt."

further swelled with the addition of several hundred season ticket holders. A very small amount of parcels traffic was also handled.

DETTON FORD

Between Cleobury Town and Stotteston on the C.M. & D.P. railway. Opened 21st November 1908 and designated a Halt from 1st October 1923, consequent upon the GWR take-over of the line. The suffix was never displayed. Single low platform, fronted with timber, having a cinder surface. Provided with a small concrete waiting shelter. Parcels traffic dealt with. Also referred to as 'Detton Ford Siding'. Closed 26th September 1938.

DETTON FORD SIDING

See Detton Ford.

DEW SIDING

Unadvertised single platform with non standard timber shelter on the Golden Valley branch between Clifford and Westbrook. Known to have been used for both goods and passenger traffic with a porter in charge until June 1924. Opened on 21st April 1889 with the name later changed by the GWR to 'Green's Siding.' Closed from 15th December 1941.

DILLWYN COLLIERY HALT

See Dillwyn & Brynteg Platform.

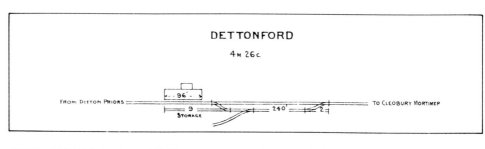

Typical of the primitive facilities on the erstwhile C.M & D.P Railway was the stopping place at Detton Ford seen here in March 1938, just six months prior to closure. This railway retained its low height platforms throughout whilst it will be noted the 'Halt' suffix was not displayed.
Roger Carpenter Collection

DILLWYN & BRYNTEG HALT

See Dillwyn & Brynteg Platform.

DILLWYN & BRYNTEG PLATFORM

Unadvertised single platform between Seven Sisters and Crynant. Used by miners from September 1928. Also referred to as 'Dillwyn & Brynteg Halt' and 'Dillwyn Colliery Halt'.

DILTON MARSH HALT

Situated between Westbury and Warminster. Authorised by the GWR on 29th October 1936, having staggered up and down timber platform 300 ft. by 8 ft, footpaths to public road, retaining wall, timber shelters, name boards, fencing, gates and electric lighting. Estimated cost of construction £1134. Opened 1st June 1937.

The down side platform at Dilton Marsh − the up side is behind the photographer. The view is looking towards Warminster; the steep gradient sometimes made it difficult for trains to re-start from the Halt.

Lens of Sutton

DINGLE ROAD HALT
See Dingle Road Platform.

DINGLE ROAD PLATFORM

Between Penarth Town and Penarth Dock on the Taff Vale Railway. Up and down platforms opened 1st March 1904 and renamed Dingle Road Halt from 2nd October 1922. Improvements authorised on 25th November 1937 consisted of lengthening the platforms from 135 ft. to 380 ft, additional waiting room, fencing and a name board. New electric lighting was also installed together with a refixed fence and fogman's hut which necessitated the re-positioning of the up distant signal. Total cost of extra work £470.

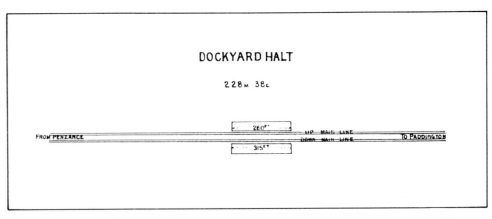

Looking west from Dockyard Halt in 1922 with an unfamiliar variation in pagoda styles visible. The buildings are apparently of the usual corrugated construction up to gutter level though the roof design is without the more normal ornate styling. This combination does not appear to have been repeated elsewhere.

LGRP

DITTON PRIORS

The terminus of the Cleobury Mortimer & Ditton Priors Railway. Opened 21st November 1908 and designated Halt by the GWR from 1st October 1923 although the title was never carried. Low platform typical of this railway with wooden station building. Although not shown on the nameboards, the Halt suffix was printed on tickets. Parcels traffic handled. Closed 26th September 1938.

DOCKYARD HALT

Sited between Devonport and Keyham. Authorised 1st March 1905 with up and down 200 ft. platforms, shelters 20 ft. by 7 ft, lamps, pathways, steps and gates to public roads at an estimated cost of £557.

Opened 1st June 1905 and reported as unstaffed by 1939 at which time supervision was exercised from Devonport.

DOCTOR DAY'S BRIDGE SIDINGS

Unadvertised stopping place used by railwaymen only, between Bristol Temple Meads and Lawrence Hill. In use by 1918 and closed some time after 1928.

DOLCOATH HALT

Situated between Carn Brea and Camborne. Up and down platforms opened 28th August 1905, closed 1st May 1908.

DOLSERAU HALT

Between Bontnewydd and Dolgelley. Single platform opened 8th February 1935 with the nameboard proclaiming 'Dolserau Halt for Terrant Walk' – a local beauty spot. See photo page 76.

DOLYGAER HALT

Single platform between Pontsticill Junction and Torpantau. Opening date not reported, but pre-1932. Unstaffed from 1932 onwards.

DONYATT HALT

Single platform between Chard and Ilminster. Opened 5th May 1928. Unstaffed and supervised from Ilminster.

A much later view of the same location, from the opposite direction. The non-standard buildings have survived.

Lens of Sutton

Late BR days at Dolygaer, which does not display the 'Halt' suffix.

Lens of Sutton

DORTON HALT

Situated between Haddenham and Brill & Ludgershall. Authorised by the GWR on 21st January 1937, consisting of up and down platforms 70 ft. by 8 ft, footpaths, steps to road, shelters, gates, fencing and electric lighting. Estimated cost of construction and facilities £374. Opened 21st June 1937.

DOSELEY HALT

Authorised on 27th October 1932 at an estimated cost of £127. Situated between Horsehay & Dawley and Coalbrookdale.

Single platform 80 ft. long with shelter and lamps. Opened 1st December 1932.

DOULTING

Unadvertised stopping place between Cranmore and Shepton Mallet. Purpose uncertain but possibly used by workers at nearby quarry. Out of use by 1906.

DOWNFIELD CROSSING HALT

Situated between Stroud and Stonehouse. Up and down platforms, opened 12th October 1903.

DRAYCOTT CAMP

Military line from Chiseldon MSWJ. Opened by September 1914 and out of use circa 1932. Further reading – The Midland and South Junction Railway, Wild Swan.

DRAYTON GREEN HALT

Situated between West Ealing and Greenford. Authorised 9th November 1904 with up and down platforms 150 ft. long with shelters and footpaths 4 ft. wide. Estimated cost £355. Opened 1st March 1905. Unstaffed, but supervised from West Ealing. For accountancy purposes receipts were

The very first 'Halts' were in the Stroud Valley, and dated from 1903. One of these was at Downfield Crossing, seen here with all the ingredients of a 'standard' halt, in the period 1903 - 1914.

National Railway Museum

included either with Southall or Greenford. 27th July 1939 extension of platforms authorised at estimated cost of £140. On 19th November 1923 the GWR Suggestions Committee records an entry relating to the 'Provision of notice boards at Drayton Green to indicate to passengers which is entrance to up and which is to down side' – marked ''Not recommended''.

DRYBROOK HALT

Terminus (the halt status was thus slightly extraordinary, though in several instances this did not deter the GWR) of the single line from Cinderford. Single platform

opened 4th November 1907. Closed 7th July 1930. Further reading – An Historical Survey of the Forest of Dean Railways, OPC.

DUFFRYN CROSSING HALT

Authorised by the GWR in February 1924

with up and down platforms 350 ft. long, shelters 20 ft. by 7 ft. and gates to roadway. Estimated cost £1078. On the GWR line between Mountain Ash and Aberdare High Level. Opened 12th July 1914, closed 2nd April 1917. Intended to serve nearby golf links and two mining villages.

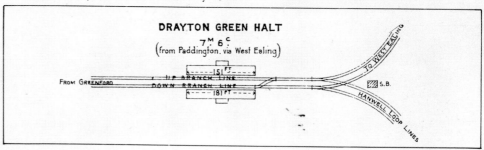

DRAYTON GREEN HALT
7ᴹ 6ᶜ
(from Paddington, via West Ealing)

A classic and almost timeless study of a Great Western halt, ironically, portrayed in 1949. This is Dolserau, utterly remote, it would seem, from any likely traffic. Despite such mischoices there was success in the 'Halt' and 'Platform' venture, which can only be gauged from the number of such stopping places which existed throughout the system.

DUFFRYN CROSSING PLATFORM

Between Mountain Ash and Aberaman on the Taff Vale Railway. Staggered up and down platforms opened in January 1905. Renamed 'Abercwmboi Platform' in February 1906 and 'Abercwmboi Halt' from 2nd October 1922. Parcels traffic handled.

DUFFRYN MILLS HALT

Believed this refers to the following entry; was an unadvertised stopping place also used by colliers.

The end at Donyatt Halt, between Chard and Illminster; rusty and weed strewn tracks unlikely to see further service. At the top right can be seen a series of tank traps, intended to slow the Germans, should they have invaded, in 1940.

Lens of Sutton

Following the demise of the steam railmotors the 48XX, later 14XX, class came to typify so many of the halt services. Even in the outer suburban area such engines could be found on auto trains, such as here at Drayton Green Halt with No. 1474 attached to trailer vehicle Wren.

Roger Carpenter Collection

Two delightful views (middle and bottom) of Drybrook Halt in the Forest of Dean showing the railway in its idyllic rural setting. From the photographs the platform is seen to have been raised in height over the years although apart from this there are few changes of note. Modellers might note the position of the various notices whilst the cultivated garden is perhaps a feature less commonly associated with 'the motor halt'.

Lens of Sutton (both)

Drybrook Halt, with the beginnings of a school outing.
Lens of Sutton

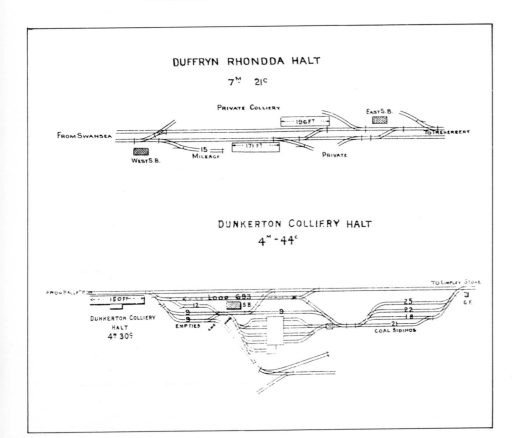

DUFFRYN MILLS PLATFORM

Unadvertised stopping place between Duffryn Junction and Bryn, consisting of a single platform. Was used from 14th February 1931 by funeral parties, on down trains only, under the control of Port Talbot Corporation. See also 'Duffryn Mills Halt'.

DUFFRYN RHONDDA HALT

See Duffryn Rhondda Platform.

DUFFRYN RHONDDA PLATFORM

Situated between Cymmer and Pontyrhydyfen on the R.H. & S.B. Railway. Staggered up and down platforms opened, unadvertised, for workmens use from about 1900 and to the public from 10th July 1905 – some reports refer to 10th July 1911. Temporary closure from 2nd October 1911 to October 1912, re-opening as 'Duffryn Rhondda Halt'. 27th October 1938 extension of platforms reported at cost of £193. Parcels traffic handled.

DUNKERTON COLLIERY HALT

Between Camerton and Dunkerton. Opened 9th October 1911 with a single

Dunkerton Colliery Halt on the Camerton branch, slightly unusual in that the word 'colliery' was publicly displayed on the nameboard. The view is looking east, towards the same name and, eventually, Limpley Stoke.

National Railway Museum

Dunsford Halt on the Teign Valley. Seen towards Exeter in its later years, in the lengthening shadows of late afternoon.

Lens of Sutton

platform 150 ft. by 8 ft. by 3 ft, surfaced with stone chippings. Standard corrugated pagoda shelter. Cost of construction recorded as £230. Temporary closure between 22nd March 1915 and 9th July 1923. Closed permanently from 21st September 1936 – some reports refer to 21st September 1925.

DUNSFORD HALT

Situated between Longdown and Christow. Opened 16th January 1928 with a single 100 ft. platform of standard height, faced with stone blocks, with an unusual corrugated shelter with sloping roof. Unstaffed, and supervised from Christow. Originally intended to have been called 'Farrents's Corner Halt.' Further reading – The Teign Valley Line, Oakwood.

DYNEA HALT

On the Alexandra (Newport & South Wales) Docks & Railway system, between Pontypridd and Caerphilly Up and down platforms formerly called Dynea, renamed from 1st July 1924. Also referred to as 'Dynes Halt'.

DYNES HALT.

See Dynea Halt.

A photograph to confuse the researcher and reader – as with Carbis Halt! The nameboard reveals 'Dunmere Halt', clearly a GWR style pagoda shelter and yet the location is not on a GWR line but instead a former LSWR route, from Dunmere Junction to Bodmin North.

Lens of Sutton

Great Western Railway Halts

E

EARDINGTON

On the single line between Bridgnorth and Hampton Loade. Opening date not reported. Originally staffed and regarded as a station hence the brick building. Date of downgrading not recorded. Halt suffix not displayed.

EAST ACCESS HALT

See Glascoed Factory East Access Halt.

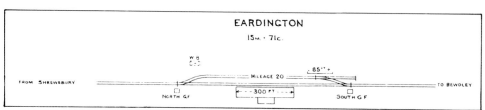

EASTBURY

Between Lambourn and East Garston. Single, originally low platform with simple timber waiting shelter. Raised in height by the GWR, consequent upon its takeover of the Lambourn Valley line. Designated a halt by the GWR although suffix was not displayed. Unstaffed by 1905. Further reading – the Lambourn Valley Branch, Wild Swan.

Eardington on the Severn Valley line between Bridgnorth and Hampton Loade. Originally a station the designation 'Halt' was given at an unknown date although as can be seen this was not displayed. The location still survives today on the preserved section of the SVR, although the station is not at present in public use.

Lens of Sutton

EAST GARSTON

Single platform between Great Shefford and Eastbury. Original low platform raised to standard height by the GWR upon take over of the line in 1905. Staffed from the outset, with parcels traffic handled. Designated a halt by the GWR although suffix was not displayed. Further reading – The Lambourn Valley Branch, Wild Swan.

EASTHOPE HALT

Between Presthope and Longville. Single platform opened 4th April 1936.

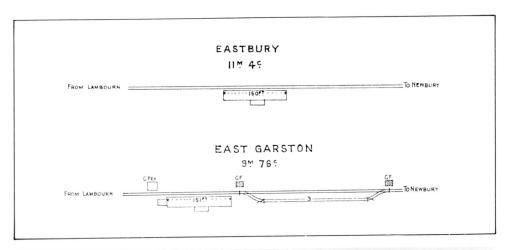

Eastbury on the Lambourn line from Newbury, looking towards the terminus at Lambourn. Regretfully no views appear to have survived showing the place in its pre-1905 state and accordingly it is not possible to detail fully the changes consequent upon the raising of the platform. The exposed nature of this 'Halt' is obvious and it could be very bleak indeed when the wind blew across the Berkshire Downs.

LGRP

EAST TWERTON HALT

4th October 1921 proposal for a halt at 'Brook Street Bridge,' one mile west of Bath station. Up and down platforms, shelters, paths to road and booking office at road level. Estimated cost of £1005. – not proceeded with.

EAST USK

Suggestion from un-named GWR member of staff, dated 31st December 1923, for a Halt at East Usk to serve the model village of Somerton Park. Comment 'not recommended'.

EBBW JUNCTION

Unadvertised stopping place between Newport High Street and Marshfield and in use by railway staff by November 1915. Abandoned by an unknown date.

EBLEY CROSSING HALT

Opened 12th October 1903, between Stroud and Stonehouse, to serve up and down trains. Originally believed to have been a 'ground level' stopping place, with standard height platforms added at a later date. 9th February 1939 electric lighting authorised at estimated cost of £113; believed installed in August 1939.

ELLERDINE HALT

Situated between Cridgington and Peplow. Up and down platforms opened 7th July 1930.

ELLIOT PIT COLLIERY HALT

Unadvertised stopping place between New Tredegar and Aberbargoed. Originally provided with up and down platforms although this was altered upon singling of the line in April 1934. In use by 1909 and later referred to as 'Elliot Pit Colliery Platform'.

The delightful stopping place at East Garston, on the Lambourn branch again, depicted c.1919. In charge of the stopping place was a 'Grade 1 Porter', who issued tickets from the wooden hut, the corner of which is just in camera. Floral displays were a feature of this location for many years.

LGRP

A very early view of Ebley Crossing Halt in the Stroud Valley, one of the first of 'Haltes' to be opened by the GWR, on 12th October 1903. There is some dispute as to which of the original stopping places were provided with low level platforms to start with and as this view dates from c.1905 the implication is that the facilities are original.

Lens of Sutton

ELLIOT PIT COLLIERY PLAT-FORM

See Elliot Pit Colliery Halt.

ELMS BRIDGE HALT

Single platform between Dingestow and Raglan. Opened 27th November 1933.

ELSON HALT

Between Ellesmere and Overton-on-Dee. Single platform opened 8th February 1937.

ERCONWALD STATION HALT

An urban halt, renamed prior to opening. See illustration at beginning – pages (ii) and (iii).

EVAILVACH HALT

Unadvertised stopping place between Ton-mawr and Cwmanan Halt. Single platform brought into use at an unknown date and out of use by 1943. Sometimes referred to as Evailfach Halt.

EVESHAM ROAD CROSSING HALT

Situated between Milcote and Stratford-on-Avon. Up and down platforms opened 17th October 1904. Closed 14th July 1916.

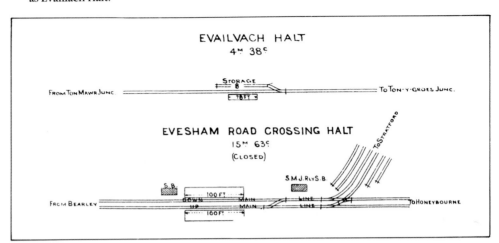

Moving ahead a few years and a number of changes are apparent at Ebley, with the addition of the pagoda and also the wooden ticket office. Access between the platforms, however, is still at track level.

Lens of Sutton

Great Western Railway Halts

F

FARLEY HALT

Between Buildwas and Much Wenlock. A single platform was provided and opened on 27th October 1934 at an estimated cost of £1260.

FARRINGTON GURNEY HALT

Situated between Hallatrow and Midsomer Norton. Single platform opened 11th July 1927.

FELIN DYFFRYN HALT

Single platform opened 10th June 1935. Situated between Trawscoed and Llanilar.

FELIN FOEL COLLIERS HALT

Unadvertised stopping place on Llanelly and Mynydd Mawr line north of Llanelly. Single platform opened by 1913 and out of use by 1929.

FELIN FRAN HALT

On the Swansea Direct Line at the junction for the Pontardaw branch. Up and down platforms opened 2nd January 1922.

FENNANT ROAD HALT

Between Legacy and Ponkey Crossing Halt. Opened 5th June 1905. Closed by 1917.

The basic arrangements at Farrington Gurney Halt, viewed in 1949, twenty two years after opening. Tickets could be purchased from the nearby Miners Arms, the path to which runs alongside the top of the cutting.

LGRP

FERNHILL COLLIERY

Unadvertised stopping place on the single track Blaenrhondda branch of the Taff Vale Railway beyond Treherbert. Dates of use not reported.

FFOCHRHIEW PITS

Unadvertised miners platform reportedly situated on the GWR/Rhymney branch from Cwm Bargoed. In use by August 1897 and closed some time after 1928. Renamed Fochriw Pits after November 1915 and Fochriw Colliery by September 1928.

FFONFRAITH HALT

Single platform on the Kerry branch from Abermule. (Sometimes incorrectly referred to by the GWR as Fronfraith.) Closed to traffic 9th February 1931.

FILTON HALT

Between Filton Junction and Henbury. Authorised on 2nd July 1909 at an estimated cost of £294. Opened 9th May 1910, closed 22nd March 1915. See also entry re North Filton Platform – later opened almost exactly on the same site. At the time of opening the 'GWR Magazine' also referred to this stopping place as Gloucester Road Halt. Further reading – Lines to Avonmouth, OPC.

Diesel railcar No. W22W at Foley Park Halt with the 8.55am Kidderminster to Tenbury Wells service – 4th March 1958. To the right are the private sidings of the British Sugar Corporation. The railway still survives at this point as part of the preserved Severn Valley line – the Halt however has long ceased to exist.

Anthony A. Vickers

The remains of Fronfraith Halt on the Kerry branch, which closed in 1931.

FINSTOCK HALT

Situated between Handborough and Charlbury. Up and down platforms authorised on 26th October 1933 at estimated cost of £362. Opened 9th April 1934. Originally to have been named 'Finstock Bridge Halt.'

FLAG STATION HALT

Opened under the name of Flag Station, between Llandderfel and Llanuwchllyn, on 14th September 1931 (although appeared in Bradshaw from 20th September 1926) and renamed Flag Station Halt 4th July 1938. Had previously, from 1868 to 1931, been the private station of Sir William Watkins-Wynn. (The name 'Flag' is said to have originated from the time guests of Sir William had arrived by train and raised a flag to summon a boat in order to travel over the adjacent lake to the home of Sir William). Originally provided with a low platform although a standard height extension was later erected at one end.

Flag Station Halt near Llandederfel, which until 1931 had been a private stopping place. The shelter is clearly of non-standard type!

LGRP

Filton Halt on the line to Henbury from Bristol, almost new, in 1909. This stopping place was destined to have a short life closing in 1915, although a replacement was later opened on almost the same site albeit under a slightly different name.

National Railway Museum

FLEUR-DE-LIS PLATFORM

South of Pengam (Mon). Up and down platforms opened 29th March 1926.

FOCHRIW PITS

See entry for Ffochrhiew Pits.

FOCHRIW COLLIERY

See entry for Ffochrhiew Pits.

FOLEY PARK HALT

Single platform between Kidderminster and Bewdley, opened 2nd January 1905 to serve nearby industrial premises.

FORD HALT

See Ford Platform.

FORD PLATFORM

Situated between Devonport and Keyham. Up and down platforms used by workmen from 1st June 1904 and at this time unadvertised. 3rd January 1906 authorisation

The delightfully named stopping place, Fleur-De-Lis Platform the literal translation of which is 'Flower'. Again the suffix is not borne on the nameboard whilst the narrow platforms have dictated the use of an equally narrow shelter, with distinctly top heavy appearance. No. 3767 is working a Newport train.

M. Hale

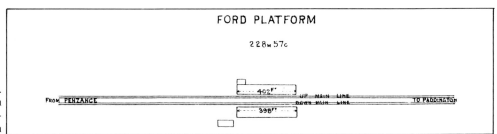

Ford, near Plymouth, the photograph originates prior to July 1922, as the name 'Platform' is carried.

Lens of Sutton

given for conversion to public use with lengthening and widening of platforms to 400 ft. and construction of new booking office and waiting room on both platforms. Public services commenced 23rd May 1906. Renamed Ford Halt 10th July 1922. Due to work on the neighbouring Keyham Viaduct, the up platform only was in use for all traffic between March 1936 and 2nd May 1937. Closed 6th October 1941.

FORGE CROSSING HALT

Single platform between Titley and Presteign. Opened 9th March 1929.

FOUNTAIN BRIDGE HALT

On the Brecon and Merthyr Railway between Machen and Caerphilly; opened in October 1908 and served by trains in the down direction only. See also entry for Waterloo Halt.

FOUR OAKS HALT

Between Newent and Dymock. Single platform opened 16th October 1937 at estimated cost of £200.

FRIAR WADDON MILK PLATFORM

Unadvertised low level stopping place, constructed of timber, and used by farmers for milk traffic between Upwey and Coryates Halt. Not known if ever used for passenger traffic. Further reading – The Abbotsbury Branch, Wild Swan.

FRONGOCH

Single platform between Bala Junction and Arenig. Halt suffix not displayed.

Fountain Bridge, in classically remote and rural setting.
Adrian Vaughan Collection

Furze Platt Halt on the single line towards Bourne End, looking back towards Maidenhead. At the end of the platform is North Town Level Crossing, a name which it had originally been intended, would be carried by the stopping place.
Lens of Sutton

FROXFIELD HALT

23rd February 1928 proposal for halt between Hungerford and Bedwyn with up and down platforms, shelters and footpaths to public road. Estimated cost of £344 – work never carried out.

FURNACE COLLIERS HALT

Unadvertised stopping place situated north of Llanelly on the Llanelly and Mynydd Mawr line. Single platform, dates of use not reported.

FURZE PLATT HALT

Single platform between Maidenhead and Cookham, authorised on 18th March 1937 at an estimated cost of £625. Opened 5th July 1937 and reduced to unstaffed status 1st November 1942. Originally intended to be called Northtown Halt. Receipts and costings included with Maidenhead Station.

FOUNTAIN BRIDGE HALT

6ᴹ 34ᶜ

FROM CAERPHILLY — 18 FT — TO NEWPORT

89

Goonbell Halt in Cornwall, depicted in 1922, boasting the customary bare simplicity of the unstaffed stopping place.

LGRP

GADLYS ROAD PLATFORM

Unadvertised miners' stopping place on the single line Dare Valley branch from Aberdare. In use by September 1928. Closed by 1948.

GAOL LANE SIDINGS

Unadvertised stopping place used by railwaymen, on the former Rhymney Railway between Cardiff Parade and Cardiff Adams Street Stations. Dates of use not reported although in September 1928 it is known a private service operated from here to the nearby East Dock locomotive shed.

GARNANT HALT

Proposal for a halt between Garnant Station and Gwaun-cau-Gurwen. Reported in 1928 as 'Not in use at present' and presumed never built.

GARDIFFRAITH HALT

See entry for Six Bells Halt.

GARNEDDWEN HALT

Between Llanuwchllyn and Drws-y-Nant. Authorised on 22nd March 1928 with up and down platforms 75 ft. long, shelters and a sleeper crossing. Estimated cost £386. Opened 9th July 1928.

GARSINGTON BRIDGE HALT

Single 150 ft. platform with shelter and path to road, between Wheatley and Littlemore. Authorised on 30th October 1907 and opened 1st February 1908; closed 22nd March 1915. Morris Cowley Station later occupied the same site, from 1928 onwards. The cost of the original facilities was a portion of £603 said to be the estimated cost of three Halts authorised at this time, viz; Horsepath, Garsington Bridge and Iffley. Further reading – The Princes Risborough, Thame Railway, OPC.

GARTH AND SUN BANK HALT

Up and down platforms between Trevor and Llangollen, opened 24th July 1905, renamed Sun Bank Halt 1st July 1906.

GATEWEN HALT

On the Wrexham to Moss branch. Single wooden platform and corrugated shelter opened 24th July 1905. Unstaffed and closed on 1st January 1931.

GELLI HALT

See entry for Gelli Platform.

Aftermath of the accident at Sun Bank Halt – formerly Garth & Sun Bank Halt on 8th September 1945, caused by a washout from the neighbouring Llangollen Canal. It overwhelmed the railway causing a train to be derailed; the driver of 2-6-0 No. 6315 was killed in the accident and the engine was cut up on the spot. The dramatic effect of the washout is apparent, with the track and embankment above supported on timber decking. In the foreground are the remains of No. 6315, whilst above an unidentified 'Dean Goods' heads a works train. The photograph was taken on 18th September 1945, ten days after the incident.

National Railway Museum

GELLI PLATFORM

Taff Vale Railway, between Ystrad (Rhondda) and Llwynypia. Up and down platforms provided from an unknown date. Unadvertised from November 1912 and known from then on as Gelli Halt.

GELLIRHAID CROSSING

This refers to an entry in the 1913 'Great Western Magazine', which declares a new halt to have been established here during 1912. It has not been possible to divine the exact location and the reference may in fact relate to the previous entry.

GETHINS PITS PLATFORM

Unadvertised miners' stopping place with staggered up and down platforms, on the single line between Castle Pit and Abercanaid. In use sometime after 1915 and abandoned by September 1928.

GILFACH FARGOED HALT

Between Pengam and Bargoed on the Rhymney Railway. Up and down platforms opened on 1st April 1908.

GILFACH GOCH COLLIERS PLATFORM

Unadvertised, at the termination of the Gilfach Branch from Hendreforgan. Brought into use in 1912.

GILFACH MAIN MOTOR HALT

The GWR 'Engineers New Works Register' of 1910 makes reference to a stopping place authorised here at an estimated cost of £720. There were to have been up and down platforms 250 ft. long, each with a waiting room, and a bridge carrying the public road over the line. The exact location is not given though it may have been near to what was later Trelewis Halt or Platform.

GLANRAFON HALT

Between Aberystwyth and Devil's Bridge on the narrow gauge line. Opened 7th May 1904 with ground level facilities. Closed 31st August 1939.

GLANRHYD HALT

On the single line between Llangadock and Llandilo. Opened sometime after June 1928.

GLARN-YR-AFON HALT

Located between Tylwch and Pantydwr. Single platform opened 16th January 1928.

GLASCOED CROSSING HALT

See entry for Glascoed Crossing West Access Halt.

GLASCOED FACTORY EAST ACCESS HALT

Unadvertised stopping place between Glascoed and Usk, serving an Ordnance Factory. Single platform in use from 3rd February 1943 and renamed 'East Access Halt' by 26th September 1949.

GLASCOED FACTORY WEST ACCESS HALT

Unadvertised stopping place situated between Glascoed and Usk and serving the Ordnance Factory. Single platform, in use from 12th June 1941.

The second Glascoed Halt, opened on 22nd April 1938, and photographed in 1949. There were several stopping places in the district with similar names.

LGRP

Site of Goitre Halt on the branch from Abermule to Kerry; it closed to passengers in 1931.

GLASCOED HALT

Between Usk and Little Mill Junction. Opened 16th May 1927 with a low ballast platform on the down side of the main line. Raised to standard height in October 1930, closed 22nd April 1938. Replaced by a new timber platform and standard pagoda shelter on the up side on 22nd April 1938.

GLASCOED ROYAL ORDNANCE FACTORY

Unadvertised stopping place on the Glascoed Royal Ordnance Factory branch from Glascoed Station. Up and down platforms in use by workmens trains from 12th December 1938, although conventional raised platforms were not provided until 2nd January 1939. Used by factory workers from 6th October 1941.

GLOUCESTER ROAD HALT

See entry for Filton Halt.

GLYN ABBEY HALT

See Pontnewydd Halt

GLYN COLLIERY SIDING

Reported located 'between Pontyberem and Cwmmawr.' Unadvertised stopping place used by miners from approximately 1898.

GLYNCORRWG/GLYNCORRWG COLLIERY

These were unadvertised stopping places on the single line of the South Wales Mineral Railway prior to the termination of that line at North Rhondda Halt. Records do not refer to the individual stopping places involved and the reader is directed to the accompanying plans. It is believed all were in use by 1928. At varying times the names of 'South Pit Halt' and 'Glyncorrwg South Pits Halt' were also used.

GLYNTAFF HALT

Between Pontypridd and Treforest Halt. Up and down platforms provided. Opening date not reported, closed 5th May 1930.

GODREAMAN HALT

On the Cwmaman branch. Single platform authorised on 31st May 1905 and opened 1st January 1906. A feature of the original stopping place was a slag built retaining wall. Closed 2nd January 1922. A replacement platform was brought into use on 2nd January 1922 on the same side of line but slightly north of the original. Closed for public use from 22nd September 1924 and reported in 1928 'Not in use at present,' implying that it may have been the intention to re-open to passengers. This was not

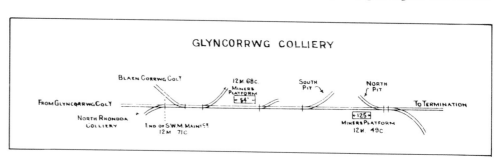

GLYNCORRWG COLLIERY

93

Gornal Halt, unkept and overgrown, in 1955, over twenty years since its last regular pasenger services. Though quietly sinking into the grass, the pagoda shelters still survive.

Roger Carpenter Collection

to be although it remained in use by miners until 1932.

GOGARTH HALT

Between Dovey Junction and Aberdovey. Single platform opened 9th July 1923.

GOITRE HALT

Single platform on the Kerry Branch from Abermule. Opening date not reported but closed to passengers from 9th February 1931.

GOLANT HALT

Single platform between Lostwithiel and Fowey. Opening date not confirmed but a temporary closure was announced from 2nd April 1917, in effect until 1st November 1917. Permanent closure from 1st January 1940.

GOLDEN HILL PLATFORM

Single platform 215 ft. long, between Pembroke and Pembroke Dock. Opened 1st July 1909. Closed 5th February 1940. Further reading – The Pembroke & Tenby Railway, Oakwood.

GOLFA

Stopping place on the narrow gauge Welshpool and Llanfair Light Railway. Closed 9th February 1931.

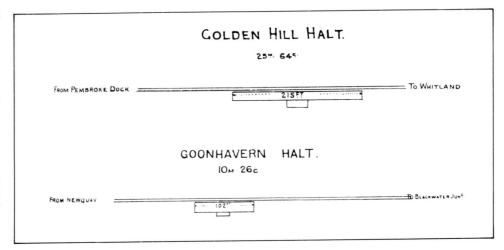

GOODRINGTON HALT

Situated between Paignton and Churston. Single platform 600 ft. by 8 ft, authorised on 20th March 1920 though not opened until 9th July 1928. Original facilities included a shelter, booking office, gate giving access to road and lighting. Estimated cost of £630. Renamed 'Goodrington Sands Halt' on 24th September 1928. Further reading – The Newton Abbot to Kingswear Railway, Oakwood.

GOODRINGTON SANDS HALT

See Goodrington Halt.

GOONBELL HALT

Single platform between St. Agnes and Perranporth. Opened 14th August 1905.

GOONHAVERN HALT

Single platform between Perranporth and Shepherds. Opened 14th August 1905.

GORNAL HALT

Up and down platforms between Brettell Lane and Himley, opened 11th May 1925. Closed 31st October 1932.

GORS-Y-GARNANT HALT

Situated between Garnant and Gwaun-cae-Gurwen. Single platform opened 1st January 1908. Temporary closure between 2nd April 1917 and 1st June 1920. Final closure came on 4th May 1926 although a Minute in 1928 implied a re-opening was possible. This did not occur.

Goonbavern in 1922, very much in the mould of Goonbell and so many others. Between Perranporth and Shepherds, as with a number of similar stopping places the 'Halt' was close to a road bridge, for maximum usage.

LGRP

GREAT ALNE

Single platform on the Alcester branch from Bearley. Originally a public station which closed on 25th September 1939. Re-opened as an unadvertised stopping place for workmen in July 1941 and finally closed 3rd July 1944.

GREAT SHEFFORD

Single platform on the Lambourn Valley line between Welford Park and East Garston. Originally supplied with low platforms and at first referred to as 'West Shefford' – renamed prior to GWR takeover in 1905. Subsequently provided with wooden shelter and staffed. Further reading – The Lambourn Branch, Pub. Wild Swan.

GREAT SOMERFORD

Situated between Dauntsey and Malmesbury, a single platform referred to in official records as a 'Halt' from 22nd May 1922, although the suffix is not believed to have been carried. Closed from 17th July 1933. Further reading – The Malmesbury Branch, Oakwood.

GREEN BANK HALT

Between Horsehay & Dawley and Coalbrookdale. Authorised on 23rd November 1933 with up and down platforms 80 ft. long, footpaths and steps to road, shelters, name and notice boards, fencing, gates, lighting and drainage. Estimated cost £283. Opened 12th March 1934.

GREEN'S SIDING

See Dew Siding.

Originally a station, Great Alne closed in 1939, to re-open as an unadvertised workmens halt between 1941 and 1944.
Lens of Sutton

A glimpse of the original low height platforms at Great Shefford, rebuilt by the GWR sometime between 1905 and 1909 – in independent days the original name of the stopping place had been West Shefford, which accounts for the alteration on the card. A 't' instead of a 'd' at the end, is however, a spelling error on the part of the original photographer.
Lens of Sutton

GREENWAY HALT

Between Dymock and Ledbury. Single platform with timber shelter opened 1st April 1937. Further reading – From Ledbury to Gloucester by Rail, Amber Graphics.

GRETTON HALT

Situated between Winchcombe and Gotherington. Up and down platforms, opened 1st June 1906.

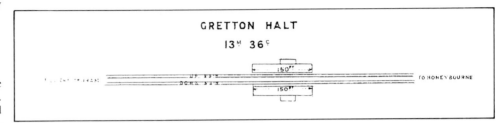

GRETTON HALT
13ᴹ 36ᶜ
150FT
UP
DOWN
150FT
TO HONEYBOURNE

Great Alne Station.

Great Sheffort Station. L.V.Ry.

Depicted some years later, Great Shefford displays all the expected trappings of a halt, without bearing the suffix.

Lens of Sutton

Great Somerford looking back to Dauntsey, its non-standard features deriving from its first days as a station. Downgrading came in 1922 and as a result supervision was exercised from nearby Little Somerford on the Badminton main line. It is not certain if a 'Halt' suffix was displayed on the nameboard. In the distance a single goods siding leads off; it was used around the turn of the century by the contractor, Pearson, who was involved in the construction of the Badminton route.

LGRP

GRIMES HILL PLATFORM

Up and down platforms opened 1st June 1908, between Shirley and Eastwood. Renamed 'Grimes Hill & Wythall Halt' from 12th July 1914, 'Grimes Hill & Wythall Platform' from 11th July 1927 and 'Grimes Hill & Wythall' from 9th July 1934. Additional (unspecified) improvements authorised on 26th January 1928 with the extension of the up side waiting room and new ladies waiting room. New lavatory accommodation was also provided, at a total cost of £330. At the same time paraffin vapour lighting was authorised for £50. Finally an additional waiting room and other unspecified accommodation was authorised on 8th October 1936, at an estimated cost of £180.

GRIMES HILL & WYTHALL

See Grimes Hill Platform.

GRIMES HILL & WYTHALL HALT

See Grimes Hill Platform.

GRIMES HILL & WYTHALL PLATFORM

See Grimes Hill Platform.

GROESFAEN COLLIERS PLATFORM

Unadvertised stopping place between Bargoed and Darran & Deri. Up and down platforms in use by September 1926. Renamed 'Groesfaen Colliery Platform' after September 1928.

GROESFAEN COLLIERY PLATFORM

See Greosfaen Colliers Platform.

GROESFFORDD HALT

Situated between Talyllyn and Brecon. Single platform opened on 8th September 1934.

GROSWEN HALT

Opening date not reported but known to have been prior to 1st July 1924. Situated between Treforest and Penrhos Junction. Provided with up and down platforms.

GWAELODWAEN COLLIERY

Unadvertised stopping place reported as sited 'between Pengam and Bargoed Colliery.' Dates of use not known.

GWAUN-CAU-GURWEN HALT

Two stopping places with this name are recorded, one at the terminus of the branch from Garnant and the other on the Cwmgorse branch, which was built but never opened. It is believed the former was 'the Halt' and was authorised on 29th September 1905 with a single platform 200 ft. by 12 ft and 'necessary shelter'; no costs are instanced. Opened 1st January 1908. Closed 4th May 1926.

A recently discovered photograph of the road approach to Great Somerford, with platform and buildings on the extreme right.

Lens of Sutton

Groesffordd Halt between Talyllyn and Brecon, the short sleeper built platform able to accommodate a single coach.

Great Western Trust

GWERNYDOMEN HALT

Situated between Machen and Caerphilly on the Brecon and Merthyr Railway. Staggered up and down platforms opened in October 1908.

GWERSYLLT HILL HALT

On the Wrexham to Moss branch. Single timber platform on the down side of the line opened 1st May 1906. No shelter provided, closed on 1st January 1931.

GYFEILLON PLATFORM

Situated between Trehafod and the Pontypridd loop on the Treherbert branch. Up and down platforms provided, closed some time after July 1918.

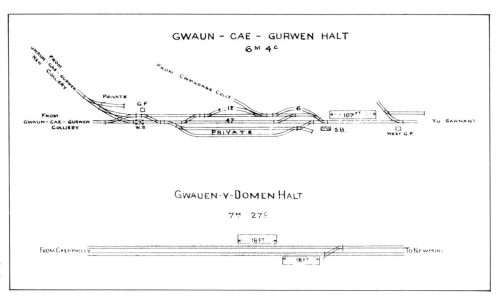

Halberton Halt, between Tiverton and Tiverton Junction, looking back towards the junction. The original intention of the railway, to provide double track, is apparent from the width of the overbridge, which affords a degree of protection from the elements.

Lens of Sutton

Ham Mill Halt, with 1472 in BR days.

W.A. Camwell

Great Western Railway Halts

H

HAFODYRYNYS PLATFORM

Authorised on 29th June 1911 at an estimated cost of £2038, the halt lay between Pontypool and Crumlin High Level. Up and down platforms 350 ft. long with booking office, 'Waiting and Retiring Room' and pathways. Contract for construction awarded to S. Robertson Ltd. for £659. (Presumably the difference between costs was to allow for items provided by the GWR). Opened 1st May 1913 – some reports refer to 1912, and unstaffed from 8th August 1932. In 1920 an un-named member of staff at the location made a comment to the GWR Suggestions Committee regarding additional lead or cement to keep out moisture from between the verandah awning and main structure. This was acted upon by the GWR although much to the chagrin of the individual who had suggested the alteration, as no gratuity was paid!

HALBERTON HALT

Single platform 109 ft. long between Tiverton and Tiverton Junction. Unstaffed with flat roofed corrugated shelter. Opened 5th December 1927. Further reading – The Exe Valley Railway, Kingfisher.

HALESOWEN

Formerly a public station on the Longbridge and Halesowen joint branch line. Unadvertised from 31st March 1928 and thereafter used by workmen.

HALLEN HALT

Between Henbury and Avonmouth. Authorised on 2nd July 1909 at a proposed cost of £235. Original platform provided on what was then the single line and opened 9th May 1910. Closed 22nd March 1915, ostensibly to release staff for war work. Re-opened as an unadvertised stopping place on 10th March 1917 with up and down platforms 700 ft. long for workmen only. Closed in October 1918 and materials from the site used at Chittening Halt. Further reading – Lines to Avonmouth, OPC.

HAM GREEN HALT

Single platform between Clifton Bridge and Pill. Authorised in October 1926 at a cost of £220. Opened 23rd December 1926. On 27th October 1927 an extension of the platform by 300 ft. was authorised together with widening to 8 ft. and provision of a shelter. Also additional lighting. Cost of work £443. Electric lighting provided in 1939 for £105.

2-6-2T No. 4110 arriving at Hafodyrynys Halt with a Pontypool Road to Neath service on the last day of operation, 13th June 1964. Bearing in mind the comments made to the GWR Suggestions Committee over the problem of water seepage between the verandah and main structure, it is likely the building depicted in the photograph had been altered somewhat since 1920.

Great Western Trust

A 1940s view of Ham Green Halt shortly after the installation of electric lighting. Notice the change in construction of the platform, an indication of the 1927 extension.

LGRP

HAM MILL CROSSING HALT

Between Brimscombe and Stroud. Up and down platforms opened 12th October 1903. Electric lighting provided in 1939 at an estimated cost of £108.

HAMPSTEAD CROSSING HALT

Proposal on 29th February 1928 for a stopping place between Newbury and Kintbury. Not proceeded with.

HAMPTON ROW HALT

Up and down platforms opened 18th March 1907, between Bathampton and Bath. Closed 25th April 1917.

HAREFIELD HALT

Between Ruislip and Denham on the Great Western – Great Central Joint line. Up and down platforms opened 24th September 1928. Renamed South Harefield Halt in May 1929. Closed 1st October 1931. Receipts included with Denham.

HAUGHTON HALT

Single platform between Baschurch and Rednall & West Felton, opened 22nd September 1934 at a cost of £250.

HAWKMOOR HALT

Situated between Bovey Tracey and Lustleigh. Single platform opened 1st June 1931.

HAYLES ABBEY HALT

Authorised on 28th June 1928 at an estimated cost of £309. Up and down platforms 100 ft. long with shelters, footpaths to road and lighting. Situated between Toddington and Winchcombe and opened 24th September 1928.

HEATH HALT

Between Cardiff and Llanishen on the Rhymney Railway. Up and down platforms 100 ft. by 9 ft. by 3ft, with shelters, opened in October 1915. Timber construction with steps on the down side and a pathway on

the up side, both leading to the public road. Inspected and approved by the Board of Trade on 6th August 1915 and at this time also occasionally referred to as 'The Heath Halt'. Renamed 'Heath Halt (High Level)' from 1st July 1924.

HEATH HALT

Between Cardiff and Whitchurch on the Cardiff Railway. Up and down platforms opened 1st May 1911 and renamed 'Heath Halt (Low Level)' from 1st July 1924. Lengthening of platforms authorised on 30th May 1935.

HEATH HALT (HIGH LEVEL)

See Heath Halt.

HEATH HALT (LOW LEVEL)

See Heath Halt

HENBURY

Opened as a public station between Charl-

Heath Halt on the Cardiff Railway system, later designated 'Low Level'. There seems, interestingly, to be only one platform, though it may have been that these were staggered, and the second is out of sight.

Lens of Sutton

A much later view of the location, after singling had taken place under BR.

Lens of Sutton

Heath Halt 'High Level' with concrete platforms and other fittings. The GWR maintained its own concrete works at Taunton although this type of material was never as widespread as on the Southern.

Lens of Sutton

ton Halt and Hallen Halt, though closed between 22nd March 1915 and 10th July 1922. During this period used as an unadvertised stopping place for workmens' trains. (After 10th July 1922 reverted to public station status).

HENDFORD HALT

Situated between Yeovil Town and Montacute. Single platform opened 2nd May 1932.

HENIARTH

Stopping place on narrow gauge Welshpool and Llanfair Railway. Previously had been referred to as 'Heniarth Gate.'

HEOLGERRIG HALT

Situated between Merthyr and Cefn Coed on the GW – LMS Joint line. Single platform, opened 31st May 1937.

HIGHTOWN HALT

Between Marchwiel and Wrexham. Single platform authorised on 12th April 1923 following a suggestion made by a member of staff from the area, who was awarded a gratuity of one guinea. Provided with shelter, footpath and wicket gates. Estimated cost of £318. Opened 9th July 1923. Also referred to as 'Hightown Platform.'

HIGHTOWN PLATFORM

See Hightown Halt.

HINKSEY HALT

Between Radley and Oxford, up and down platforms with shelters and paths to road; opened 1st February 1908 at an estimated cost of £417. Closed 21st March 1915.

HIRWAUN FACTORY HALT

See Hirwaun Trading Estate.

HIRWAUN POND HALT

Situated between Hirwaun and Rhigos Halt. Up and down platforms provided. Date of opening not reported – but see next entry.

Displaying a number of SR features, Hendford Halt near Yeovil served an industrial site as well as a residential area.

Lens of Sutton

A rare view of the short lived Hinksey Halt, during a time of severe flooding in the Oxford area. A number of 'motor halts' were provided in the area although some failed to attract the necessary patronage and were quickly closed. The site was later obliterated with extensions and alterations to the track layout.

L. Waters Collection

HIRWAUN TRADING ESTATE

Reported as situated on R.O.F. branch at Hirwaun Pond. Unadvertised stopping place, believed in use from 23rd July 1941. There is some confusion between these Hirwaun sites; the 'unadvertised halt' may well be the 'Hirwaun Factory Halt.'

HORFIELD PLATFORM

Between Ashley Hill and Filton Junction. Up and down platforms with booking office on one side and alcove on the other, authorised on 29th April 1926. Opened 14th May 1927 and renamed Horfield from November 1933.

The second Horspath Halt, which dated from 1933. From track level a good view is obtained of the timber staging supporting the platform and pagoda shelter.

LGRP

A close up of the nameboard at the Horspath Halt, supported by old rails. Notice also the lamp standard, clearly not a Swindon design and probably made of old tube for cheapness.

Lawrence Waters

HORSPATH HALT

Single platform 150 ft. long, with shelter, between Wheatley and Littlemore. Authorised on 30th October 1907 and opened 1st February 1908; closed 22nd March 1915. On 23rd March 1933 authorisation was given for another halt of the same name (these places were notable, if only for the confusion sown) on a site a few yards east of the original location. This was constructed at an estimated cost of £200 and opened on 5th June 1933. Facilities in this second case were a timber platform, corrugated pagoda shelter and cinder path leading down to the access road. From June 1933 receipts were included with those from Morris Cowley Station.

HOTWELLS HALT

On the Clifton Extension Joint Line, between Sea Mills and Hotwells. Opened 14th May 1917. Closed 3rd July 1922. Further reading – Lines to Avonmouth, OPC.

HUNNINGTON

Unadvertised stopping place between Halesowen and Rubery on the GW/MR joint line. Previously a public station which was subsequently allowed the patronage of workmen only, from April 1919.

The platform at Ilton Halt, the pathway in the next view leading in from the right.

Lens of Sutton

A view not usually recorded – the access path to a halt – in this case at Ilton, on the Chard branch. The wooden structure appears to be a waiting room; it stood on the bank side, due to lack of space at the platform.

Lens of Sutton

Ingra Tor on the Princetown branch, one of the most exposed of all halts and sidings.

Roger Carpenter Collection

Great Western Railway Halts

I

IDE

Situated between Alphington Halt and Longdown. Single platform originally a station but downgraded to Halt status some time prior to June 1928. Further reading – The Teign Valley Line, OPC.

IFFLEY HALT

Single platform 150 ft. long, with shelter, opened 1st February 1908 between Littlemore and Oxford. Approximate cost £201. Closed 22nd March 1915. A note in the records reveals the original name proposed for this location to have been 'Oxford Sewage Bridge Halt'.

ILMER HALT

Situated between Princes Risborough and Haddenham on the Great Western – Great Central Joint. Up and down platforms, opened 1st April 1929. Receipts included with Haddenham.

ILTON HALT

Single platform between Ilminster and Hatch, opened 26th May 1928.

INGRA TOR HALT

Single timber platform with wooden shelter opened 2nd March 1936. Between Dousland and Princetown. Further reading – The Princetown Branch, OPC.

Downgraded from a station prior to 1928, Ide was one of the stopping places on the picturesque Teign Valley line, between Exeter and Newton Abbot.

Lens of Sutton

Jackfield Halt, in typical 'edge of town' location, in 1952. Notice the wheel within the finial of the distant signal, which allowed the lampman to lower it to the ground, avoiding the need to climb to the top of what was a particularly high post.

Lens of Sutton

Great Western Railway Halts

J

JACKAMENT'S BRIDGE HALT

Situated between Kemble and Culkerton. Single platform devoid of shelter, opened 3rd July 1939 to serve Kemble aerodrome. Further reading – The Tetbury Branch, Wild Swan.

JACKFIELD HALT

Between Coalport and Ironbridge & Broseley. Single platform opened 3rd December 1934 at an estimated cost of £192.

JORDANSTON HALT

Up and down 'facilities,' consisting of sleepers at rail level brought into use on 1st October 1923. Situated between Mathry Road and Fishguard. Further reading – The Railways of Pembrokeshire, H.G. Walters.

The roofs beyond Jackfield Halt indicate the steep slope on which it stood; it was later moved, in face of a threatened landslip.

Lens of Sutton

Jackfield Halt. Almost all of the construction is in timber though comparison of the various views will reveal a change to concrete fence posts.

Lens of Sutton

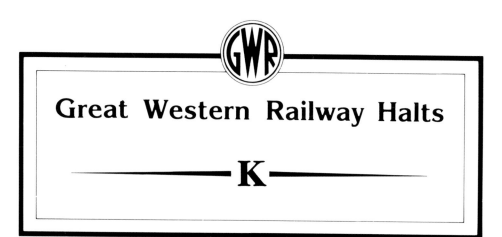

Great Western Railway Halts

K

KELMSCOTT AND LANGFORD HALT

Single platform between Alvescot and Lechlade, opened 4th November 1907, sometimes referred to as Kelmscott and Langford Platform although neither suffix was displayed. Further reading – The Fairford Branch, Oakwood.

KETLEY TOWN HALT

Single platform between Ketley and Lawley Bank. Opened 6th March 1936.

KEYHAM ADMIRALTY PLATFORM

On private branch from Keyham GWR, single platform serving the naval dockyard. In use by 1867.

KIDWELLY FLATS HALT

Unadvertised stopping place with up and down platforms situated between Kidwelly and Lando Platform. Reported first used in 1940, serving the R.A.F. Pembrey camp.

KIDWELLY QUAY

Unadvertised stopping place reported as situated on the BPGV branch from Trimsaran road. Used by miners at unknown dates.

KELMSCOTT AND LANGFORD PLATFORM

20M 25c

FROM FAIRFORD   F A I R F O R D   B R A N C H   TO OXFORD

300FT

An awful day at Kelmscott and Langford in 1934. Originally a station, it was downgraded to a 'Halt' after 1928, though the designation was not displayed. The view is towards Fairford.

Mowat Collection

Retaining its low height platform until closure, Kingston Crossing Halt took its name from the nearby level crossing, which can be seen at the end of the platform.

LGRP

KINGSTON CROSSING HALT

5ᴹ 8ᶜ

FROM WATLINGTON   TO PRINCES RISBOROUGH

⊢ 70FT ⊣

Hikers at King Tor platform on the Princetown Branch.

Lens of Sutton

KINGSTEINGNTON HALT

1923 reference in the GWR Suggestions Committee Minutes for a Halt near Newton Abbot, to meet road competition – 'Not recommended'.

KINGSTON CROSSING HALT

Situated between Chinnor and Aston Rowant. Single low platform opened 1st September 1906. Traffic receipts included with Watlington. Further reading – The Watlington Branch, OPC.

KINGSWEAR CROSSING

See entry for Kingswear Level Crossing.

KINGSWEAR LEVEL CROSSING

Unadvertised stopping place between Churston and Kingswear. Single platform used by naval personnel from 1877 onwards. A shelter is known to have existed in later years. At varying dates also known as 'Britannia Halt,' 'Kingswear Crossing,' and 'Steam Ferry Crossing.' Further reading – The Newton Abbot to Kingswear Railway, Oakwood.

KING TOR HALT

Situated between Dousland and Princetown. Single platform of gravel topped earthwork, edged with timber. Wooden shelter provided. Opened 2nd April 1928. Despite being officially classified a 'Halt' the nameboard proclaimed 'Platform'! Further reading – The Princetown Branch, OPC.

Great Western Railway Halts

L

LACOCK HALT

Between Chippenham and Melksham. Up and down platforms, opened 16th October 1905.

LAIRA HALT

Up and down platforms opened 1st June 1904, between Plympton and Plymouth. On 29th July 1926 authorisation was given for a subway instead of the existing footbridge, at an estimated cost of £620.

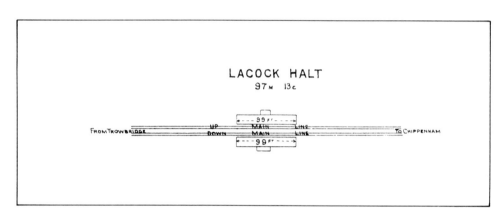

Lacock Halt and First Motor, opened oct. 16, 1905.

'The first train to call at Lacock Halt, on 16th October 1905'. The formation is certainly unusual, a steam railmotor, siphon van and then a locomotive. Notice the low height platforms provided at this time.

Lens of Sutton

Nearly fifty years later at Lacock Halt, with a 69XX series 'Hall' steaming through on a westbound passenger train. To the left are Lacock sidings, whilst in the distance it is just possible to glimpse the controlling signal box.

B.J. Miller

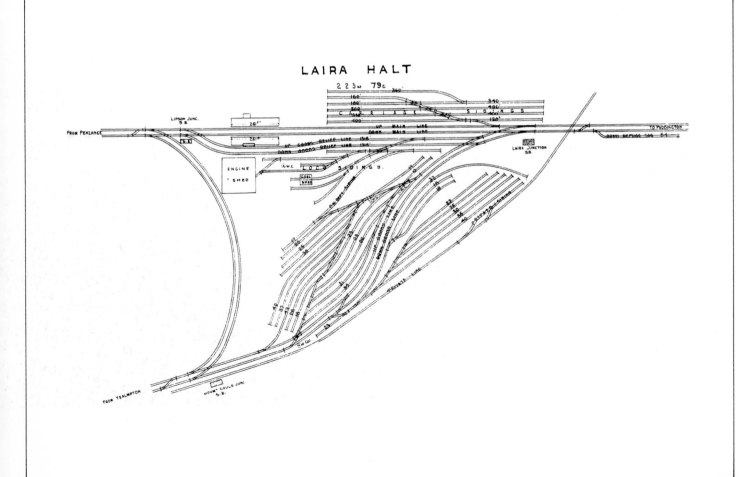

A pre-1926 view of Laira Halt with the footbridge, which was later superseded, and engine shed, in the background. To the right would appear to be the photographer's cape and case.

LGRP

LAIRA HALT. G.W.R.

Busy times at Laira Halt with a pair of steam railmotors and sandwiched coach on a down working. In the right background it is just possible to discern the shed coaling stage and what may well be a 'Dean goods' 0-6-0.

LGRP

LANDO HALT

See entry for Lando Siding.

LANDO PLATFORM

See entry for Lando Siding.

LANDO ROYAL ORDNANCE FACTORY/LANDO R.O.F. PLATFORM

On the R.O.F. line west of Lando Halt. At least two separate single platforms, at different locations were in use, the first some time between 1915 and 1932 and the second probably from 24th February 1942. It is suggested a third platform (details unknown) may have been provided by October 1945.

LANDO SIDING

Unadvertised stopping place between Pembury & Burry Port and Kidwelly, with up and down platforms serving an explosives works; in use by November 1915. Name changed at an unknown date to 'Lando Halt' and to 'Lando Platform' by September 1928.

LAVERTON HALT

Up and down platforms 100 ft. by 7 ft. by 3ft, each provided with a shelter 20 ft. by Toddington and passenger access was via a 1 in 8 ramp, leading down to a road underbridge. There was also a sleeper crossing at the north end. On 2nd August 1905 the GWR informed the Board of Trade of its intention to construct the stopping place, which opened to the public on 14th August 1905. This was followed by a further letter on 6th September 1905, declaring the arrangements ready for inspection; Colonel Yorke attended on 16th October 1905 and found everything in order. In certain documents the stopping place is referred to as 'Laverton Motor Halt.'

LEDBURY TOWN HALT

Single platform between Dymock and Ledbury. Opened 26th November 1928. Further reading – From Ledbury to Gloucester by rail, Amber Graphics.

LEGACY

Single platform on the Rhos branch south of Rhostyllen. Opening date not stated and classified as a halt, though no suffix was carried. Reported that parcels traffic was handled.

The line from Ledbury to Gloucester was clearly built for double track; witness the width of the overbridge and the single platform of Ledbury Town Halt, in the position that would have been occupied by the second line of rails.

Roger Carpenter Collection

Lecknor Bridge Halt on the Watlington branch, in 1919, probably little changed from the time of opening in 1906. This stopping place retained it low height platform throughout its life.

LEWISTOWN HALT

Between Pontyrhyll and Pontycymmer. Single platform opened 10th August 1942.

LEWKNOR BRIDGE HALT

Between Aston Rowant and Watlington. Single platform opened 1st September 1906. Access by steps to road under bridge.

LIDDATON HALT

Single platform on the north side of the line, opened 4th April 1938. Situated between Coryton and Lydford.

LIGHTMOOR PLATFORM

Up and down platforms constructed of timber and opened 12th August 1907. On the

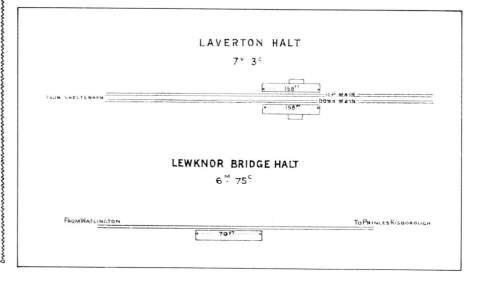

up side facilities consisted of a corrugated waiting room and ladies room whilst on the down side were booking office and parcels office, at road level. Lying between Horsehay & Dawley and Coalbrookdale, the stopping place was staffed with two 'Grade 1' porters under the supervision of the Coalbrookdale Station Master. Note: some uncertainty exists over the opening date; according to R.A. Cooke a station had existed at this location by 1880. Was 1907 then the date of downgrading? Temporary closure between 1st January 1917 and 7th July 1919.

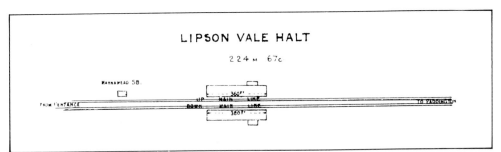

LIPSON VALE HALT

Situated between Plympton and Plymouth, up and down platforms opened 1st June 1904; they were shortened around March 1933 and the location closed on 22nd March 1942.

LITTLE DRAYTON HALT

Authorised on 25th July 1935 at an estimated cost of £240 between Tern Hill and Market Drayton. Up and down platforms opened 14th September 1935.

LITTLE STRETTON HALT

Situated between Church Stretton and Marsh Brook on the Shrewsbury and Hereford Joint. Up and down platforms, shelters, etc. provided at an estimated cost of £302. Opened 18th April 1935.

LLAFAR HALT

Between Arenig and Trawsfynydd. Single platform authorised on 27th October 1932 at an estimated cost of £108. Opened 1st March 1932.

Close up detail of the timber shelter at Liddaton halt, opened in 1938. Illumination appears to have been by oil lamps, which would be lit and extinguished by the train guard.

Lens of Sutton

Lightmoor Platform, on the main line from Wellington. In this view the trestle supports to the platform are clear, as is the extra length pagoda, unusual and thereby strange to the eye.

Roger Carpenter Collection

From the platforms the overall timber construction of the Lightmoor stopping place is apparent, making good use of redundant sleepers. Generally these would have a topping of tarmacadam; this was intended to prevent creosote, rising to the surface from within the wood, being carried into trains on passengers' shoes.

Mowat Collection

A 1922 view of Lipson Vale Halt near Plymouth, looking west. The narrow platforms were later shortened, around 1933.

LGRP

LLANABER HALT

Between Barmouth and Dyffryn Ardudwy on the Cambrian Railway. Opened in July 1914.

LLANBADARN HALT

On the narrow gauge Vale of Rheidol line from Aberystwyth. Ground level, and not believed to have carried the halt suffix. Further reading – The Vale of Rheidol Light Railway, Wild Swan.

LLANBETHERY PLATFORM

Single platform between St. Mary Church Road and St. Athan Road. Opened 1st May 1905 and closed 12th July 1920. Reported in 1928 'Not in use at present'. Further reading – The Cowbridge Railway, OPC.

LLANBRADACH COLLIERY HALT

Situated on the Bassaleg Junction and Rhymney line. Up and down platforms, unadvertised and in use by September 1928.

LLANDANWG HALT

Between Llanbedr & Pensarn and Harlech. Single platform opened 8th November 1929.

LLANDARCY PLATFORM

Authorised on 27th March 1924 with up and down platforms 200 ft. long, approach roads, shelters and retaining walls, lamp hut, booking and parcels office. Estimated cost of £1706. Opened 22nd September 1924, the halt lay between Briton Ferry and Llangyfelach.

Llandogo Halt in the Wye Valley. The nameboard fails to display the suffix – that underneath is an advert for The Daily Telegraph. Aside from the shelter and lamps the only other item of furniture would appear to be a fixed board beyond the hut, used to display a timetable of services.

Lens of Sutton

Another shelter variation was provided at Llanfaredd Halt here, apparently, in BR(W) two tone chocolate and cream livery.

Lens of Sutton

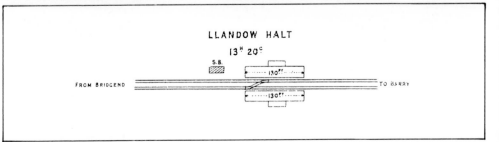

LLANDARCY PRIVATE PLATFORM

See entry for Londas South Private Platform.

LLANDAVEY HALT

O.S. Nock makes reference to this location in his 'History of the GWR Part 3, 1923-48,' giving its closure as 4th October 1947. No details as to location or opening dates have been found.

LLANDECWYN HALT

Single platform between Talsarnau and Penrhyndeudraeth. Opened 7th July 1930, although certain reports refer to 18th November 1935, at an estimated cost of £150.

LLANDOGO HALT

Between Tintern and St. Briavels. Single platform opened 9th March 1927. (The nearby St. Briavels station subsequently had the suffix 'for Llandogo' dropped from its name).

LLANDOUGH PLATFORM

Between Grangetown and Cogan. Staggered up and down platforms opened at an unreported date and closed prior to 1947.

LLANDOW HALT

On the Barry Railway, between Llantwit Major and Southerndown Road. Staggered up and down platforms opened 1st May 1915.

LLANDOW (WICK ROAD) HALT

Situated between Llantwit Major and Southerndown Road. Up and down platforms opened 19th April 1943.

Llangower Halt with basic facilities, though it boasts a standard station seat. Such luxury was certainly not usual and any seating seldom amounted to more than a sleeper, supported at each end.
LGRP

A view of Llangorse Lake Halt, retaining for the present (though clearly due for replacement) its timber platform. The photograph is looking north, in 1950.
LGRP

LLANERCH-AYRON HALT

Between Cilliau Aeron and Aberayron. Single platform opened 2nd October 1911.

LLANFABON ROAD HALT

See Llanfabon Road Platform.

LLANFABON ROAD PLATFORM

Opened 1st November 1904, between Traveller's Rest and Nelson on the Taff Vale Railway. Renamed 'Llanfabon Road Halt' from 2nd October 1922. Closed 12th September 1932.

LLANFAREDD HALT

Situated between Builth Wells and Aberedw. Single platform opened 7th May 1934.

LLANGELYNIN HALT

Single platform opened 7th July 1930, between Tonfanau and Llwyngwril.

LLANGOLLEN ROAD HALT

Situated between Chirk and Cefn. Up and down platforms opened 1st October 1905. Renamed Whitehurst Halt from 1st May 1906.

LLANGORSE LAKE HALT

Single platform between Trefeinon and Talyllyn Junction. Opened on 9th July 1923 at an estimated cost of £242.

LLANGOWER HALT

Between Llandderfel and Llanuwchllyn. Single platform with corrugated iron shelter opened 10th June 1929.

LLANGYBI

Single platform between Derry Ormond and Olmarch Halt on the Aberystwyth branch. Opening date not reported and though designated a halt it is not believed to have carried the suffix. Parcels traffic handled.

LLANION HALT

150 ft. single platform with small shelter opened 1st May 1905; situated between Pembroke and Pembroke Dock. Closed 1st October 1908. Further reading – The Railways of Pembrokeshire, Pub. H.G. Walters.

LLANSTEPHAN HALT

Between Erwood and Boughrood & Llyswen. Single platform opened 6th March 1933.

LLANYBLODWELL

Single platform on the Tanat Valley Branch. Designated a halt though suffix probably not displayed.

LLWYDCOED

Situated between Gelli Tarw Junction and Abernant. Authorised on 26th May 1910 with a single platform 200 ft. long at an estimated cost of £600. Entry in the records at this time was one of four referring to '...Extension of the rail motor service in the Vale of Neath area with additional Halts....,' dated 26th May 1910. The others were Cwmbach Halt, Pontwalby Halt and Rhigos Halt. Llwydcoed however does not appear to have been granted halt status at this time and unlike the other locations does not appear in the 1928 list of halts.

LLYS HALT

Between Llanuwchllyn and Drws-y-Nant. Single 70 ft. platform with shelter opened on 4th June 1934 at estimated cost of £120.

LODGE HALT

Between Wrexham and Brymbo, 38 chains from the former station. Up and down timber platforms each with a shelter. Although unstaffed a small wooden hut was provided for the issue of tickets on Saturdays when it was considered necessary for a porter to be present. Opening date not reported but prior to 1924. Note: referred to in certain documents as 'The Lodge Halt.'

Another halt put up on the ground intended for a second line of rails was Llanstephan, where the road over the bridge clearly shows the formation width available. Notice the pathway leading up to the roadway as well as the lack of any obvious lighting.

Lens of Sutton

LONDAS SOUTH PRIVATE PLATFORM

Situated, according to official records, between Court Sart and Llandarcy Platform. Used by workmen from 7th July 1919 until 4th May 1925. Name changed to 'Llandarcy Private Platform' around 1923.

LONG ASHTON PLATFORM

Between Bedminster and Flax Bourton. Authorised on 26th November 1925 with up and down platforms 400 ft. by 10 ft, corrugated iron shelter and lamp hut on up side, pathways and gates. Booking office provided on the path leading to the up side. Estimated cost £1930. Opened 12th July 1926. Parcels traffic reported to have been handled. 'Platform' suffix dropped from 23rd September 1929. Closed to all traffic from 6th October 1941.

LONGBRIDGE

Unadvertised stopping place on the joint GWR/MR Longbridge and Halesowen branch south of Rubery. Up and down platforms used by workmen from February 1915.

LONGDON HALT

Situated between Wellington and Crudgington. Authorised 4th October 1934 with up and down platforms 100 ft. long, shelters, name and notice boards, fencing and lighting. Estimated cost £290. Opened 20th October 1934.

LONG SUTTON & PITNEY

See photograph opposite.

LOWER LODES HALT

23rd January 1947, proposal for a new halt between Powerstock and Bridport, to serve the villages of Upper and Lower Lodes. Intention was to have a concrete trestle platform 150 ft. long, concrete shelter and other necessary works. Estimated cost £1045. For an unknown reason this work was not carried out.

LOWER PENARTH HALT

Situated between Cadoxton and Alberta Place Halt. Up and down platforms originally opened as a station in 1897 and reduced to halt status from February 1934.

LOWER SOUDLEY

See photograph opposite.

LOWERY HALT

1908 proposal for a halt on the Princetown

branch between Princetown and Dousland.

LYNG HALT

Between Durston and Athelney. Single platform opened 24th September 1928.

LYDSTEP HALT

See entry for Lydstep Platform.

LYDSTEP PLATFORM

Situated between Penally and Manorbier. Single platform originally opened as an unadvertised stopping place for excursion traffic circa 1897; became public with the name 'Lystep Halt' from 1st May 1905. Temporary closure between 21st September 1914 and 9th July 1923. Closed from 22nd January 1934.

This ends the first half of *Great Western Halts*, alphabetically A – L. Those halts lettered M – Y appear in Volume Two.

In attempting to compile a register of stopping places designated 'Halts' there are bound to be anomalies; here is one, Long Sutton & Pitney. Architecturally it would certainly appear to be appropriate to this book although it does not appear in official 'Halt' listings. The view is looking west, towards Somerton. No opening date is reported.

Lens of Sutton

Another anomaly concerns 'Lower Soudley Halt' on the GWR Forest of Dean branch from Newnham. Although it fails to appear in official records various railway books refer to a stopping place at this point, and this would appear to be confirmed by the small platform, visible just ahead of the steam railmotor. It is not certain if this was used by passengers or merely goods traffic.

Lens of Sutton

With a mixture of concrete and timber fittings, Lyng is perhaps a typical example of a later 1920s halt, where economy was of ever greater importance. The solitary fire bucket is slightly amusing, the stopping place being unstaffed.

Lens of Sutton

G. W. R. Standard Platform & Shelter for Halts, Lighting.

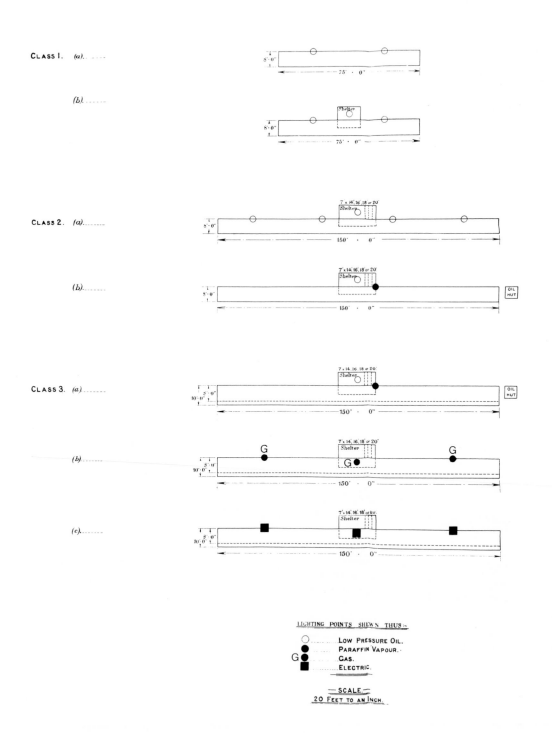

CLASS 1. (a).

CLASS 1. (b).

CLASS 2. (a).

CLASS 2. (b).

CLASS 3. (a).

CLASS 3. (b).

CLASS 3. (c).

LIGHTING POINTS SHEWN THUS:—

○ .... LOW PRESSURE OIL.
● .... PARAFFIN VAPOUR.
G● .... GAS.
■ .... ELECTRIC.

—SCALE.—
20 FEET TO AN INCH.

Appendix One

In 1927 J.C. Lloyd, the GWR Chief Engineer, wrote of the standard fixtures and fittings to be provided at stopping places: on 7th November he set out a memorandum detailing the facilities of a 'standard halt...'

As it has been noticed that schemes for new halts vary in dimension as to width of platforms and size and type of shelter, I have been in correspondence with the Superintendent of the Line with a view to standardisation. As a result it has been agreed to standardise the following:-
Platform width: 8ft 0ins
Shelter: corrugated iron – 12ft 0ins x 8ft 0ins or 20ft 0ins x 7ft 0ins according to traffic requirements, as to which the Divisional Engineer must consult the Divisional Traffic Superintendent.

A little later, on 27th July 1928, Lloyd wrote again, on the construction of the platforms, mentioning also two plans, reproduced in this section – the recipient of the letter is not stated:

Construction of Halt Platforms. Referring to correspondence which has from time to time arisen in regard to construction of halt platforms of standard height, enclosed I send you two prints ... shewing two standard types of construction for general adoption.

(a) This shews the construction for platforms where the ground is level or in a cutting and in the latter case usually the concrete post and wire fencing at the back of the platform need not be provided. If, under special circumstance, in cuttings you still consider it desirable to fix this fencing, please clearly state the reason in the letter which accompanies your estimate.

(b) The construction shewn on this print is for use on embankments or where the halt is in the nature of an experiment and may, within a comparatively short period, be required to be moved to another site. The serviceable sleeper decking shewn should be regarded as the normal construction, but where the halt may be regarded as a permanency, on occasions it may be considered desirable to use new timber decking. When this is povided for in your estimate please clearly state the reason in the letter which accompanies the estimate.

The next letter came on 26th September 1928, again to an unnamed Officer ...

Ramps at Halt platforms: Recently a question was raised as to the necessity for providing platform ramps with a gradient of 1 in 8 as specified in the Ministry of Transport Requirements at halts where the ramps would not be required to be used either by passengers or for the transport of luggage. The question has been referred to the Ministry of Transport who has agreed that in such cases a gradient of 1 in 4 may be accepted subject to inspection. If, therefore, you have instructions to provide any halts at the present time, please consult the local Traffic Officers as to the use which will be made of the ramps and if any of them will not be used by passengers or for luggage these should be constructed to gradients of 1 in 4 with strips of wood or other suitable non-slipping devices fixed at suitable intervals. This will also apply in the case of any halts authorised in future for which plans and estimates have already been submitted, but in the case of other future halts, the matter must be gone into with the local Traffic Officers previous to submitting your plan and estimate and where 1 in 4 ramps are shewn, please state definitely in your accompanying letter that the ramps will not be used by passengers or for luggage. It must be clearly understood that whenever there is likelihood of the ramps being used by passengers or for luggage the existing Ministry of Transport minimum gradient of 1 in 8 must be adhered to.

Drybrook Motor Halt.

The Halt as rural idyll. Drybrook, retouched by the artist.
Collection Brian Hilton

The final item of correspondence found is dated 13th August 1936 and is again on the subject of standard platforms and shelters for halts. By this time it was R. Carpmael, who had taken over from Lloyd as Chief Engineer in 1929 ...

Referring to Minute No. 890 of the Engineers' Conference held on the 30th January last, enclosed I send you a specification which I have drawn up in respect of standard platforms and shelters for the various classes of halts, having shown against each item the figures which are to be used in future when estimating for normal cases.

The prices shown for Class A platforms are for halts on level ground and include necessary notice and trespass boards, but excluding any preparation of the site, levelling etc. and formation of approaches. The amounts for lighting also are for lights on the platform, and in the shelter if provided; they do not cover lighting or approaches. Where a platform is provided on an embankment the additional cost in supporting the platform must be added. Costs are in each case given for a single platform.

On single lines, ramps at both ends to be 1 in 6. Where two platforms are required and passengers will cross the line on the level the slope of the ramp at each end of the crossing to be 1 in 8 (or 1 in 10 if Parcels etc. traffic is anticipated, involving a crossing of the line).

In the case of Class B platforms here also the figures shown do not cover excavation or other preparatory works at the site, and except as shown the cost will be the same as for Class A platforms.

I attach a print showing the lighting covered by my estimate for each type of halt.

Specification:

1. THAT OF CHEAPEST POSSIBLE CONSTRUCTION for use in sparsely populated districts, constructed of serviceable timber for platforms and supports, or with supports of Taunton concrete trestles, width 8ft length 75ft. Nameboard to be of light construction with posts cut out from serviceable sleepers. £60.
Shelters, 12ft x 7ft if required, to be of light timber construction without door, coated with Cuprinol inside and out, except seats (to be painted) Roof to be of corrugated iron or of boards covered with Ruberoid. Price includes one oil lamp. £24.
Oil Lighting £12.
Oil hut only specially asked for £16.

2. GENERAL TYPE, with platforms 8ft wide, length 150ft constructed of and supported on serviceable timber or supported on Taunton concrete trestles. Lettering on name boards to be Preswood or similar material. £96.
Shelter to be of timber without doors, coated with Cuprinol inside and out, except seats (to be painted).
Size 7ft x 14ft £24; 7ft x 16ft £27; 7ft x 18ft £33; 7ft x 20ft £35 as required. Roof to be of boards covered with Ruberoid with valance as on Standard Drawing.
Oil £27 or Petrol Vapour Lighting £18.
Oil hut for petrol vapour lighting only unless specially asked for with oil lighting £15.

3. SPECIAL TYPE for use in districts which have already been developed or which are rapidly developing. Precast concrete trestles (running front to back only) with concrete lamp, fence and name board posts. Lettering on name boards to be Preswood or similar material. New timber deck treated on all faces with Cuprinol. Platform widths 8ft £118, to 10ft, £145 as required by Traffic Department, length 150ft.
Shelter to be of timber treated with Cuprinol inside and out, except seats (to be painted). Size 7ft wide x 14ft £24; 7ft x 16ft £27; 7ft x 18ft £33 or 7ft x 20ft £35 as required by Traffic Department. Roof of shelter to be of boards covered with Ruberoid with valance as on standard drawing.
Petrol Vapour £18.
Coal Gas £40 or Electric lighting £45.
Oil hut for petrol vapour lighting £15.

Halts of all types situated in cuttings will be constructed with sleeper walls or Taunton concrete slabs and coping, with back filling covered with slag screenings, which in classes 2 and 3 should subseqently be tar sprayed. Type 1 £60.
Type 2 £96.
Type 3 8ft wide £96 10ft wide £106.
For estimating purposes 10% contingencies to be added.
The estimates for gas and electric lighting do not cover charges for service connections which the Company may be called on to pay, and they assume that mains exist adjacent to the site of the Halt. Where these mains are set at a distance the necessary amounts should be added.

Appendix Two

Number of Halts and Platforms opened 1903-1947, including joint lines. As given in Clinker's **Register**.

HALTS							PLATFORMS					
1903	4	1918	0	1933	25		1904	1	1910	1	1918	1
1904	13	1919	0	1934	22		1905	1	1911	2	1924	1
1905	51	1920	0	1935	16		1906	4	1912	1	1925	2
1906	22	1921	0	1936	9		1907	3	1913	1	1926	5
1907	13	1922	2	1937	10		1908	7	1915	1	1927	2
1908	11	1923	6	1938	5		1909	1				
1909	3	1924	5	1939	5							
1910	6	1925	8	1940	0							
1911	10	1926	4	1941	1							
1912	7	1927	11	1942	2							
1913	2	1928	28	1943	2							
1914	3	1929	26	1944	0							
1915	1	1930	15	1945	0							
1916	0	1931	12	1946	0							
1917	1	1932	14	1947	1							

Platforms and halts opened by companies taken over by the GWR and still in use at the date of absorption:

Barry	1
Brecon & Merthyr	3
Burry Port & Gwendraeth Valley	3
Cambrian	4
Cardiff	4
Rhymney	4
Rhonnda & Swansea Bay	2
Taff Vale	15

Note — the above does not include; locations classified as halts or platforms and not carrying the suffix, downgradings, and private or untimetabled stopping places.

Appendix Three

TRAFFIC DEALT WITH AT STATIONS.

Station	Year	Staff — Supervisory and Wages No.	Staff — Paybill Expenses £	Total Receipts £	Tickets Issued No.	Season Tickets No.	Passenger Receipts including S.T., etc. £	Parcels & Misc. Number	Parcels & Misc. Receipts £	Total £
Ashton Gate Platform.	1929	Included with Clifton Bridge,		1,548	Included with Clifton Bridge	Included with Clifton	1,527	prior to 1926. 285	prior to 1926. 21	1,548
	1930			1,460	39,616	7	1,420	285	21	1,460
	1931			1,361	36,384	14	1,308	553	40	1,361
	1932			1,234	33,019	12	1,194	843	53	1,234
	1933			1,299	30,560	13	1,246	799	40	1,299
	1934			1,289	33,077	12	1,228	178	53	1,289
	1935			1,289	39,579	3	1,225	2,812	61	1,289
	1936			1,271	37,497	15	1,195	3,206	64	1,271
	1937			1,545	38,087	23	1,433	3,842	76	1,545
	1938			1,512	42,436	11	1,388	4,439	112	1,512
					37,664			4,411	124	
Bathford Halt.	1929	Included with Bathampton.		273	March, 1929.	March, 1929. 3	273	—	—	Opened March, 1929. 273
	1930			347	11,466	16	347	—	—	347
	1931			315	15,095	17	315	—	—	315
	1932			315	14,665	17	315	—	—	315
	1933			320	13,731	23	320	—	—	320
	1934			373	13,380	32	373	—	—	373
	1935			357	15,172	29	357	—	—	357
	1936			254	14,962	26	254	—	—	254
	1937			217	9,415	26	217	—	—	217
	1938			227	6,809	13	227	—	—	227
					6,584					
Box, Mill Lane Halt.	1930	Included with Box.		826	March, 1930.	March, 1930. 125	811	313	15	Opened March, 1930. 826
	1931			1,065	15,339	185	1,048	290	17	1,065
	1932			1,071	19,308	237	1,061	200	10	1,071
	1933			1,044	17,687	218	1,034	176	10	1,044
	1934			1,003	15,555	203	993	140	10	1,003
	1935			1,062	14,283	228	1,056	142	6	1,062
	1936			1,016	14,439	247	1,006	207	10	1,016
	1937			1,128	13,001	244	1,117	192	11	1,128
	1938			1,241	14,532	278	1,233	113	8	1,241
					16,687					
Chiseldon Camp Halt.	1930	Included with Chiseldon.		203	December, 1930.	December, 1930. 184	203	—	—	Opened December, 1930. 203
	1931			1,028	1,076	—	1,028	—	—	1,028
	1932			1,097	1,355	—	1,097	—	—	1,097
	1933			871	1,156	with Chiseldon after 1933.	871 after	1933.	—	871
	1938			Included with Chiseldon						Included
Collingbourne Kingston Halt.	1932	Included with Collingbourne		105	April, 1932.	April, 1932. 3	105	—	—	Opened April, 1932. 105
	1933			153	1,311	5	153	—	—	153
	1934			142	1,896	8	142	—	—	142
	1935			157	1,715	24	157	—	—	157
	1936			154	1,536	13	154	—	—	154
	1937			149	1,245	10	149	—	—	149
	1938			126	1,450	6	126	—	—	126
					1,231					
Coryates Halt	1929	Included with Upwey.		293	Included with Upwey after 1934.	—	—	—	293	293
	1930			405	—	—	—	—	405	405
	1931			544	—	—	—	—	544	544
	1932			901	—	—	—	—	901	901
	1933			837	—	—	—	—	837	837
	1934			100	—	—	—	—	100	100

TRAFFIC DEALT WITH AT STATIONS.

STATION.	YEAR.	STAFF. Supervisory and Wages (all Grades). No.	STAFF. Pay Bill Expenses. £	TOTAL RECEIPTS. £	Tickets Issued. No.	Season Tickets. No.	Passenger Receipts including S.T. etc. £	Parcels and Misc. Number. No.	Parcels and Misc. Receipts. £	Total. £
Farrington Gurney Halt.	1929		Included with Hallatrow.	Opened July, 1927	9,306	32	553	—	—	553
	1930			553	7,670	15	417	—	—	417
	1931			417	7,398	20	379	37	37	416
	1932			416	6,214	27	337	523	275	612
	1933			612	5,954	32	352	1,626	200	552
	1934			552	4,996	32	314	406	48	362
	1935			362	5,401	47	368	—	—	368
	1936			368	5,911	48	363	—	—	363
	1937			363	6,360	48	420	—	—	420
	1938			420	5,637	65	411	—	—	411
Great Somerford Halt.	1903	5	191	2,565	8,666	..	588	22,306	1,574	1,862
	1913	4	213	1,464	6,641	..	410	19,731	581	991
Ham Green Halt.		Included with Dauntsey.		Included with Dauntsey. Closed July, 1933.	Included with Dauntsey after 1922.					
Hewford Halt.	1929		Included with Pill.	Opened December, 1928. Included with Pill after 1932.	139		107			107
	1930			107	114		204			204
	1931			204	69		199			199
	1932			196	56		258			258
	1933			258			342			342
Horfield Platform. (†)	1929	†	†	Opened May, 1925.	May, 59,621	1925. 154	1,671	631	33	1,704
	1930			1,704	74,488	217	2,054	715	46	2,080
	1931			2,080	80,331	230	2,217	685	41	2,258
	1932			2,312	71,287	280	2,281	542	31	2,312
	1933			2,835	76,995	302	2,793	649	42	3,129
	1934			3,126	82,277	325	3,074	847	48	4,065
	1935			3,496	87,278	288	3,448	898	57	4,643
	1936			4,065	102,902	332	4,015	937	52	
	1937			4,643	100,029	362	4,586	1,031		
	1938			5,478	100,029		5,466	1,164		
Ide Halt. (†)	1903	2	52	Included with Exeter (St. Thomas)	May, 5,276	..	101	740	16	117
	1913	2	112		7,782	..	190	1,795	83	273
	1923	1	275		7,819	6	233	557	22	255
	1929			869	10,422	5	270	584	59	329
	1930			596	10,435	8	282	745	33	321
	1931			538	8,691	19	253	758	35	288
	1932			465	7,149	26	244	709	33	277
	1933			439	6,351	16	226	846	37	263
	1934			515	5,270	36	192	869	20	212
	1935			548	4,394	57	177	204	16	193
	1936			563	3,819	73	174	174	17	191
	1937			398	3,244	84	174	164		
	1938			329						

GOODS TRAIN TRAFFIC.

STATION.	YEAR.	Forwarded. Coal and Coke "Charged." Tons.	Forwarded. Other Minerals. Tons.	Forwarded. General Merchandise. Tons.	Received. Coal and Coke "Charged." Tons.	Received. Other Minerals. Tons.	Received. General Merchandise. Tons.	Coal and Coke "Not Charged" (Forwarded and Received). Tons.	Total Goods Tonnage. Tons.	Total Receipts (excluding "Not Charged" Coal and Coke). £	Livestock (Forwarded and Received). Wagons.	Total Carted Tonnage (included in Total Goods Tonnage). Tons.
Farrington Gurney Halt.	1929			112	512	489	538	445	2,053	733		110
	1930			68	403	621	556	478	2,126	473	1	135
Great Somerford Halt.												
Ide Halt.	1903		36	62		26	80	6	122	75		46
	1913			411	10	1,208	100	133	2,020	530	3	66
	1923	12		302	49	623	136	94	1,100	490	3	22
	1929			425		2,917	100	270	3,411	541	1	51
	1930			78	40	1,639	56	241	948	210	0	16
	1931			59		261	75	273	1,229	177	3	19
	1932			53	45	59	73	167	662	162	7	30
	1933			59		45	86	120	407	252	5	30
	1934			124		33	62	170	414	336	4	13
	1935			64		62	49	160	373	361	3	8
	1936			73		16	23	124	357	205		
	1937			95		60		56	399			
	1938								154